W9-CNM-312

Danger and Opportunity

Danger and Opportunity

Resolving Conflict in U.S.-Based Japanese Subsidiaries

Clifford H. Clarke and G. Douglas Lipp

INTERCULTURAL PRESS, INC.

Intercultural Press
P.O. Box 700
Yarmouth, Maine 04096 USA
207-846-5168

Book design and production: Patty J. Topel
Cover design: Patty J. Topel

Printed in the United States of America

02   01   00   99   98   1   2   3   4   5

Library of Congress Cataloging-in-Publication Data

Clarke, Clifford H.
    Danger and opportunity: resolving conflict in U.S.-
based Japanese subsidiaries/Clifford H. Clarke and G.
Douglas Lipp.
        p.   cm.
    ISBN 1-877864-59-5
    1. Corporations. Japanese—United States—Manage-
ment.   I. Lipp, G. Douglas.   II. Title.
HD70.U5C542   1998
658.4'053—dc21   98-4939
                                                      CIP

Table of Contents

Acknowledgments

As I look back through time, I find that there are a significant number of friends and family members to whom I owe my deepest gratitude for their respective strengths which sustained me through this first effort to share my understandings of the complex business environment between Japanese and Americans in the United States. To David S. Hoopes for going far beyond the role of editor in helping me to formulate ideas through dialogue and to structure them appropriately; to G. Douglas Lipp for his initiation of this project and his tenacity in urging us to its conclusion; to Joseph Bellon for his principal role in questioning, recording, and writing drafts of so many creative sessions we spent together; to my sister, Jennie E. Clarke, for caring for me through a prolonged battle with mercury poisoning during the time when most of the writing had to be done; to Muneo Yoshikawa, former Professor at the

University of Hawaii, for his insight on the interaction of these two cultures which he shared with me in the trenches of several projects; to Harumi Befu, retired Professor at Stanford University, my mentor throughout most of my PhD (ABD) program; to Roger Fehrina, formerly of the Procter & Gamble Company, who took me under his wing for two years and taught me about business operations during my first major consulting project; to Shinji Susaki, my boss during my first Japanese employment thirty-six years ago, who gave me the total immersion experience at the Hotel Okura in Tokyo; and finally to my deceased parents, Jabe and Coleman D. Clarke, without whom I would never have had the incredible experience of growing up in Japan (or anywhere else for that matter!), I express my deepest appreciation. I hope that through this work they can see their own contributions to this bridge-building process between our two cultures.

—Cliff Clarke
January, 1998
Kamula, Hawaii

Acknowledgments

I dedicate this book to my family. The constant love and support of my wife, Pam, and my children, Allison, Amanda, and Keith, gave me the energy to continue. They gave up a lot of family time without me over the last eight years. Thank you. It is also important to thank my parents, Gordon and Pauline Lipp, for their love and guidance. They introduced me to the joys and benefits of living in an international environment.

Of course, there are many other people in Japan and the United States who have been an inspiration to me. Specifically, my many friends at the Nagoya YMCA who provided guidance and my colleagues at the Oriental Land Company, Tokyo Disneyland, and NEC Corporation who shared so much business insight.

A special friend and mentor is Mr. Jun Akishige, now retired from the Nagoya YMCA. Akishige-San and his family first welcomed me into their home many years ago. My life and research in Japan would not have been possible without their kindness.

Condensing large volumes of data into a useful format is a herculean task requiring endless patience and energy. David Hoopes, editor-in-chief of Intercultural Press, provided just the right balance of knowledge, assertiveness, and care to keep this project on track.

—Doug Lipp
January 1998
Sacramento, California

Note from the Authors

The working title of this book was simply *Kiki*, 危機, which means "crisis" in Japanese. We chose that title because it represents the situation facing many U.S.-based Japanese companies today. These companies are often characterized as being ideal marriages of the best aspects of Japanese and American cultures. The reality in many cases, however, is that some of the worst aspects of each culture—or, at least, those elements which cause conflict through mutual misunderstanding—end up as the dominant influences in U.S.-based Japanese companies. These cross-cultural conflicts constitute a relatively serious threat to successful corporate operations, and this threat is presently strong enough to warrant the use of *Kiki*. But there is more to *kiki* than meets the eye. The two characters or sounds that make up the word have a different meaning if read independently of each other. The first *ki* character 危 means "danger." The second *ki* character 機 means "opportunity." Thus, within every crisis situation lies some element of opportunity as well as danger.

It is in this juxtaposition of danger and opportunity that we wish to suggest ways of dealing with the conflicts and misunderstandings that are occurring between Japanese managers and their American employees in U.S.-based Japanese companies—and, indeed, between local and global operations wherever they may be.

Frustration, anger, miscommunication, decreased productivity, lawsuits, and increased employee turnover—all these dangers are inherent in the clash of cultures that is taking place. There is, however, an alternative to the current conflict: Americans and Japanese can seek out mutually acceptable strategies for working together. That is the opportunity within the danger. Pursued diligently and with good faith, the chances of success are great. It is the purpose of this book to provide a tool or vehicle for that pursuit and to entice Japanese and American managers, supervisors, and employees of U.S.-based Japanese companies to examine together the elements of danger and opportunity already at work in their companies.

The greatest danger lies in simply ignoring the profound differences between the two cultures. Predictable patterns of mutually misunderstood behaviors are presented in this book, and we challenge you to compare the issues we examine with the situation in your own company. The most important opportunity lies in recognizing the problem areas and resolving to do something about them. This puts you in a better position to work as a team to develop a stronger organization, one that has the potential to take the best of both cultures and form a more effective hybrid business culture.

It is important to note that the potential for serious cross-cultural conflict in the workplace is not limited to interactions between Americans and Japanese. As the world becomes "smaller," and marketplaces everywhere begin to take on global characteristics, managers will increasingly find themselves presented with the challenges of a multicultural working environment. In the following chapters we will focus on conflicts in U.S.-based Japanese subsidiaries, but the lessons we have learned about cross-cultural conflict are potentially applicable to a much wider range of multicultural work settings.

Part One

Framework for Analysis

Introduction

I n this book, we take a unique approach to examining the challenges that emerge from the vastly different management styles of Japanese and Americans. In addition to describing and comparing differences, we offer solutions to the problems that arise from them. We methodically examine the most frustrating problem areas faced by Japanese managers and their American subordinates in U.S.-based Japanese companies. Each topic is analyzed in depth, and strategies for problem solving and conflict resolution are provided.

We have attempted to write this book in a format which is easy to understand and follow. Using case studies derived from actual situations, we lead the reader through a series of steps designed to get at both the causes of and the solutions to key cultural conflicts. This analysis is based on our forty combined years of direct, professional experience in researching, consulting, and training Japanese and Americans to work productively together in the United States and Japan. In each of the cases the authors served as consultants to management in working through its problems within the framework of our seven-step conflict resolution model.

Research undertaken by the authors on U.S.-based Japanese subsidiaries has identified eight areas in which Japanese and American managers say their business styles most often clash. These are (1) work habits, (2) training and development, (3) responsibility and authority, (4) promotion pace and compensation growth, (5) performance management and equal employment opportunity, (6) information management and decision making, (7) positive and negative feedback, and (8) communication style.

According to a 1997 report by the U.S. Department of Commerce, there are 3,241 Japanese subsidiaries in the United States, employing over 758,000 Americans.[1] There are two reasons why these numbers are so large. First, the number of Japanese companies looking for overseas sites multiplied dramatically during the last decade. This was due in large part to the rising cost of labor and real estate in Japan; the higher value of the yen against the dollar; the demand for better customer service in the United States; and tariffs, quotas, and other possible sanctions on imports. The second reason for the rise of Japanese companies in the United States is that during the 1980s, most states and municipalities set up formal economic development organizations whose sole purpose was to identify and attract Japanese and other Asian companies to their areas. Many of these programs were quite successful.

In spite of widespread economic difficulties in both countries in the late 1980s and early 1990s, the cheap dollar helped the spread of Japanese companies into the United States. In

---

[1] *Survey of Current Business*, "Foreign Direct Investment in the United States" (July 1997) Washington, DC: United States Department of Commerce.

fact, the recession in Japan actually forced more companies into establishing foreign subsidiaries. Now, on the other hand, fiscal conservatism by state governments in the United States has exhausted funds for Japanese-oriented economic development organizations, and cost-cutting measures by American companies have made it more difficult for Japanese subsidiaries to invest in expansion and still remain competitive. Nevertheless, because of constantly fluctuating yen/dollar values and other factors, the number of U.S.-based Japanese subsidiaries continues to grow.

We chose to write about this topic for two reasons. First, the large number of Japanese companies in the United States means a great deal of Japanese-American interaction, which results and will continue to result in friction between the American and Japanese business communities and, very likely, between the United States and Japan in general. Second, there is an urgent and increasing need among managers and employees in these companies for resources which will help them clarify and resolve disruptive clashes in the workplace. This need is particularly acute during times of economic hardship. Cultural conflicts that are routinely smoothed over when a company is doing well financially can escalate into company-wide crises when times are tough and nerves are frayed. The decline in morale and productivity which results from culture-based conflicts is also viewed with a more critical eye by company managers when the bottom line is felt to be less secure. Now, more than ever, there is a mandate for lasting, effective resolution of cultural conflicts.

In recent years, information about U.S. and Japanese business relations has become far more available. It can generally be divided into three categories: (1) superficial information about how to do business with the Japanese, (2) analyses of the Japanese style of management and how it can be either emulated or surpassed by American corporate leadership, and (3) analyses of the impact on the United States of U.S.-based Japanese subsidiaries, primarily in the area of manufacturing.

This information has come in every conceivable form, from books, magazines, and newspaper articles to television specials, the Internet, and videotapes. Superficial information about how to do business with the Japanese is usually targeted at the American businessperson who is either relocating to Japan or who is in some way trying to conduct business with the Japanese. Much of it has focused on negotiation strategies and such things as business card etiquette and other professional and social dos and don'ts. Analyses of the Japanese style of management have covered a number of topics, ranging from quality-control circles and statistical process control strategies to consensus management. Only recently, in response to their increasing numbers, have we seen analyses of the impact of U.S.-based Japanese subsidiaries on the United States. This category consists of studies (both supportive and critical) of (1) the economic impact various subsidiaries have had on their local communities; (2) the extent to which a previously displaced workforce has been revitalized; (3) the effect of the well-publicized Japanese manufacturing systems of total quality control, just-in-time (JIT) supply management, and *kaizen* (continual pursuit of perfection) on the productivity of the American worker; and (4) management and labor/union relations under the Japanese in comparison to more traditional American models.

Although these publications and studies are valuable and have provided a great deal of information, there is a critical area which has been overlooked to date: the quality of the interface between Japanese and American cultures in the workplace. Nor has there been much effort to provide practical, tested methods of making the interface successful. What can the Japanese do to become more effective managers of Americans, and what can Americans do to be more competent in dealing with Japanese management? In this book, we will discuss conflicts which are both cross-cultural and intercultural in nature—that is, we will discuss conflicts which arise from the differences between Japanese and American cultures as well as conflicts which arise from the *interaction* that takes place between the two cultures in the workplace and in social settings.

Some Japanese companies in the United States attempt to operate under a policy they call "Americanization" or "localization." Others attempt to transfer Japanese management styles and systems to the American workplace, such as was done at New United Motor Manufacturing, Inc. (NUMMI) between Toyota and General Motors. Regardless of the approach, very few (if any) companies are doing anything about managing culture, about examining the impact of culture-based attitudes and behaviors in workplace relationships and processes. A few articles have been written on the subject, and there has been the occasional story about a strike here or there. However, little has been said about the day-to-day frustrations that occur between Japanese management and its American subordinates in the workplace, whether it's automobile manufacturing, trading companies, banks, or the electronics industry. In particular, the manual on how to improve the quality of these relationships is missing.

In Japanese subsidiaries most of the employees (including midlevel managers) are American, while top managerial positions are usually filled by Japanese expatriates. During their assignment in the United States, these Japanese executives face the dual tasks of conducting business according to the structures of the parent company in Japan and managing a workforce which has vastly different notions of management-subordinate relations. On the other side, the American subordinates, used to the cultural norms governing employer-employee relations in the United States, are faced with the challenge of carrying out their duties in a Japanese environment they don't fully understand. Both often end up frustrated and angry, and the consequences range from mutual Japan/America bashing and the erection of defensive communication barriers to high turnover and, in the end, lawsuits.

Language barriers are often blamed for these kinds of problems. But it is no secret that merely speaking each other's language does not guarantee effective or efficient communication in a business environment. The root of the problem goes much deeper than language differences. Despite the English fluency of his Japanese boss, one American manager of technology in a Japanese company had this blunt comment: "Working with the Japanese grows more and more dislikable. I just don't like them very much. It's frustrating. We don't really understand where the bumps are, why we have problems. They assume we are dumb. We assume they are stupid."

More often, problems arise because of the differing cultural expectations and assumptions each side has regarding management style and subordinate behavior. The common sense rules of the game, as understood by one side, are not the same common sense rules understood by the other. These kinds of expectations are driven by the value system of the society in which one grows up. When these so-called common sense behaviors are not displayed, those who expect them react negatively. This is what led one Japanese senior manager to say of his American management team, "I can't trust them because they set goals which are ridiculously low and easy to achieve, yet they complain that I set goals which are impossibly high. I think you call what they are doing 'sandbagging,' don't you?" The Japanese manager is looking for certain types of behavior he has come to expect from subordinates in Japan. Likewise, the American subordinates are looking for certain behaviors they have come to expect from their previous non-Japanese superiors. In many cases, neither side gets what it is looking for. The result: the high turnover rates and discrimination suits noted above. In one Silicon Valley company, turnover reached 40 percent before something was done to correct the problem. In other cases, Americans have filed suits over being denied promotion opportunities. In one New York City-based company, six women sued for gender discrimination.

These are no small matters, and they call for a new

approach on the part of both the Japanese and the Americans. What is needed is a managerial style and an organizational atmosphere which foster the blending of cultural perspectives and draw strength from differences in culture-based behaviors and attitudes. The alternative to this new style is festering conflict and hostility that can only sap the energy of the organization. The answer lies in what is being identified today as a global approach to corporate management. This does not imply the imposition of a strongly centralized "corporate headquarters" way of doing business in the rest of the world. Multinational corporations have spread around the world in complex networks, employing vast numbers of people from different countries and with different cultural backgrounds. In our opinion the global approach to corporate management does imply the balancing of cultural dynamics between head-quarters and subsidiaries or other partners. This great global diversity of business cultures creates an imperative no corporate leader can ignore and a new fact of economic life that corporate personnel, especially at the supervisory or management levels, will have to come to terms with. In the following chapters, we will lay out what we believe is a framework for understanding and dealing with these issues. Armed with this new knowledge, we hope that Americans and Japanese working in U.S.-based Japanese companies can move ahead into the future, confident in their ability to manage the stresses inherent in cross-cultural operations. We also hope that this analysis will serve as a model for examining and dealing with cultural conflicts involving other countries and cultures.

A caveat before going on. You will find in the text not only many generalizations about American and Japanese cultures but the articulation of blatant stereotypes as well. These come directly from the conflicts described and reflect the feelings of the Japanese and Americans involved—as derived from interviews and observation. They are, thus, the essence of what the authors were trying to mediate and do not reflect the authors' own views.

2

The Seven-Step
Conflict Resolution Model

The conflicts examined in this book are taken from actual incidents which have occurred in U.S.-based Japanese corporations. In each case, the authors were called in as consultants to assist in resolving the problem. It is our intent here to provide the reader with the results of that experience and with a clearly defined framework of problem analysis so that the strategies we recommend can be easily understood and effectively applied in the workplace. This book is designed for both Japanese and Americans. In it, we will lead the reader through a series of steps which provide a model for resolving cultural conflicts. Our goal is to help readers understand each problem from both the Japanese and American viewpoints, establish common objectives, and then move together toward an effective resolution.

Resolution of cultural conflicts in the workplace takes

time, and the strategies must be carefully thought through. Effective conflict resolution is not about mimicking the management style practiced by the headquarters in Japan or demanding things be done the "American way." Instead, the resolution is worked out through a process of negotiation between the employees and management of each culture. Working toward mutual understanding of cultural values and identifying appropriate behaviors and policies for the binational organization are challenges that require patience and reason. But how is that actually done? The answer—through an interactive cross-cultural (in other words, intercultural) conflict resolution process.

In addition to discussing differences between Japanese and Americans, we have introduced strategies for bridging those differences when the two cultures interact. In everyday life, organizations experiencing cultural conflict often turn first to lectures by university professors, advice from attorneys, or books by popular cultural commentators. Although possibly rich in information, this approach can lead to disappointment because people are not necessarily able to put into practice what they only read or hear. What they need is the ability to actively implement new interactive approaches. The decision on which approaches to use must balance knowledge building with skill building. Information which focuses primarily on acquisition of knowledge about the differences between Japanese and American cultures is not sufficient. The key component in helping people become more effective at working across cultures is to give them opportunities to practice new communication and behavioral skills with people from the other culture. This results in the acquisition of both knowledge *and* skills.

In order to accomplish this goal, Japanese and Americans will need to better understand how culture affects the way they view themselves and each other, how it defines their expectations of each other, how it governs their reactions to each other, and, in the end, how it all too often produces very negative perceptions of each other. They will need to learn how managers and subordinates can stop their negative perceptions from escalating into workplace conflict and then how to resolve differences when conflict does occur. To some this may sound complicated, difficult, and unlikely to succeed, so let us state it more simply. The ultimate objective of this book is to explore the issues and help people work them out in mutually acceptable ways. This involves the following principles, which constitute a conceptual framework for what we are trying to accomplish.

1. Anthropology teaches us that people are affected by the standards and norms of the society in which they grow up, live, and work. The result is what we call culture, which consists of values and beliefs, ways of behaving, patterns of thinking, and styles of communication which generally characterize the members of a culture and which are neither inherently good nor inherently bad.

2. Each of us is, of course, a unique individual with our own special ways of thinking, behaving, valuing, and communicating—and our own special beliefs as to what is right and wrong, natural or unnatural, and acceptable or unacceptable. Nevertheless, despite our individual uniqueness, the culture in which we have grown up (and been acculturated) influences us so strongly that we can identify common values and patterns of thinking and behaving which are shared by large numbers of any national, linguistic, religious, gender, generational, socioeconomic, ideological, or ethnic group. This is true of the Japanese, perhaps especially so because of their relative homogeneity, and of Americans, despite the fact that the population of the United States is large and diverse. Beyond the cultural differences are the universals which provide the framework within which we recognize each other as human beings. Nonetheless, as we all have seen, even such a basic concept as the definition of human rights is not universal, except as we try to impose it on other cultures.

3. The best way to manage is the way that gets the best results. In U.S.-based Japanese companies, the best results usually come from a blending of the perspectives and practices of the two cultures. This approach allows members of both cultures to come closer to a realization of their full potential and produces positive results at both the interpersonal and the organizational levels.

Although cultural differences lie at the heart of many of the conflicts and clashes which occur in U.S.-based Japanese companies, at the same time, these very differences constitute a valuable resource for finding creative solutions to organizational problems. *The tendency of managers to deny cultural differences and to presume universal truths when attempting to manage groups of people in organizations is the number-one barrier to organizational effectiveness in multinational corporations.* Comments such as the following are often heard: "There are no differences really. In the end, we are all striving for the same thing," or "Common sense is our best guide." As a result of our investigation of intercultural issues in the U.S.-based Japanese subsidiaries with which we've worked, our method of inquiry has yielded us hundreds of critical incidents that were identified by the members of the subject organizations as embodying the misunderstanding and conflict caused by culture-based differences in behaviors and values. From these, we have chosen eight case studies which illustrate the most significant conflict-generating issues that we have encountered. Further, each case represents one of eight major characteristics of all organizations. These are modifications of the original Seven "S's" developed by McKinsey & Company and discussed by Richard Pascale in his book *The Art of Japanese Management* (NY: Simon & Schuster, 1981). Note also that the characteristics and their case studies are the chapter titles for chapters 3 through 10.

1. *Corporate Values:* chapter 3
   Case Study: Work Habits

2. *Business Strategies*: chapter 4
   Case Study: Training and Development

3. *Corporate Structure*: chapter 5
   Case Study: Responsibility and Authority

4. *Staffing Policies*: chapter 6
   Case Study: Promotion Pace and Compensation Growth

5. *Performance Standards*: chapter 7
   Case Study: Performance Management and Equal Employment Opportunity

6. *Operational Systems*: chapter 8
   Case Study: Information Management and Decision Making

7. *Job Skills*: chapter 9
   Case Study: Positive and Negative Feedback

8. *Professional Style*: chapter 10
   Case Study: Communication Style

In each chapter, we will do two things: (1) describe a critical incident, focused on a real event in a real company, which illustrates the kinds of cross-cultural conflicts which occur in American-based Japanese subsidiaries, and (2) follow the action taken in each incident through the steps of our conflict resolution model. This model is one which the authors have used successfully with many teams of Japanese and American managers to assist them in developing mutually acceptable strategies to overcome their intercultural problems.

Our experience leads us to believe that the best management style for U.S.-based Japanese companies is one that blends the perspectives and practices of the two cultures. Quite simply, it gets results. If the best way to manage is the way that gets results, then a process that has been tested and applied effectively in a wide variety of corporate settings—the process we will describe in the remainder of this chapter—could be of significant value to anyone concerned with making cross-cultural management a success. Because we make it clear every step of the way that culture is the root cause of the conflict, it might seem that we are portraying cultural diversity as an obstacle to effective corporate operations. On the contrary, diversity is essential in creating the leading-edge strategies and alternative solutions that enhance a company's competitive capability. Rather than casting culture as the villain, the purpose of this conflict resolution process is to bring culture out into the open so that it can become an organizational strength. Valuing cultural diversity in the workplace will lead to greater harmony, more creativity, and stronger organizational identity, which in turn will enhance an organization's productive teamwork and its leadership in the marketplace, both locally and globally.

To achieve the goals we have set forth, we offer the following seven-step process through which each of the eight issues of cultural conflict will be discussed.

Seven-Step Problem-Solving Model
 1. Problem Identification
    A. Statement of the Problem
    B. Description of the Incident
 2. Problem Clarification
    A. Comparative Intentions
    B. Comparative Perceptions
 3. Cultural Exploration
    A. Hidden Cultural Expectations
    B. Hidden Cultural Assumptions and Values
 4. Organizational Exploration
    A. Global Imperatives
    B. Local Conditions
 5. Conflict Resolution
    A. Achieving Harmony

B. Goal Setting

C. Strategic Transition Planning

D. Action Planning and Implementation

6. Impact Assessment

A. Monitoring Results

B. Modifying the Plan

C. Assessing Benefits

7. Organizational Integration

A. Recording Results

B. Celebrating Achievements

C. Institutionalizing Benefits

We will use this seven-step process as a guide to assist us in describing the nature and resolution of the key issue of cultural conflict presented in each chapter. Further, to enhance the value of the model as a conflict resolution tool, we have included in the first five steps the description of a number of specific *facilitation strategies* which human resources (HR) or organizational development staff can use in implementing the conflict resolution process.

A critical element in applying these strategies and, indeed, in pursuing the aims of the conflict resolution model as a whole, is the creation of an effective bicultural team of facilitators or trainers consisting of both Japanese and Americans. The bicultural team can be made up of facilitators who are employees of the company, outside consultants, or a combination of the two. In the authors' experience, internal facilitators are most often found in the human resources or organizational departments, but the input of frontline and operations personnel must be considered to ensure a balanced approach. In order for such a team, whether internal or external, to be effective, team members must not only have an extensive knowledge base in the other culture but also need to have had prolonged contact with or experience in it. It is especially valuable for the Americans to have spent a significant amount of time at the subsidiary's headquarters in Japan. In addition, when internal facilitators are used, it is imperative that they be objective and sensitive to the needs of both cultural groups.

The Japanese members will have to understand English, while the Americans, even if they don't speak Japanese, should be very familiar with Japanese communication styles.

The necessity of the facilitation team being bicultural lies in the fact that no matter how knowledgeable of and experienced in each other's culture and/or how well they speak each other's language, the facilitators will still approach their assignment from their own cultural perspective and act on the basis of culturally conditioned biases of which they may be unaware. Nevertheless, the bicultural team offers the best way to fuse these differences in perspective into effective conflict management.

For example, failure to consider these criteria caused trouble in one U.S.-based Japanese company. Two well-intentioned American human resource managers attempting to resolve conflict actually aggravated the problem by being insensitive to the needs of the Japanese. These HR managers were approached by a group of American operations managers who complained that their Japanese counterparts were not sharing enough information with them. This, they claimed, limited their ability to make good, timely decisions. The American HR managers decided to conduct a needs assessment and, recognizing that some of the Japanese were weak in English, had the questionnaire translated into Japanese. Armed with these questionnaires, the Americans conducted a series of data-gathering meetings, first with the Americans, which produced a wealth of information, and then with the Japanese, which resulted in far less information and only one suggestion for resolving the problem: that they, the Japanese, needed to improve their English language skills.

After analyzing the information, the American human resources staff decided to bring the two groups together to "hammer out an agreement." They asked the participants to be frank and open and to "put their cards on the table." Participation in the meeting was dominated by the American managers, who shared their feelings and suggested solutions. The Japanese said relatively little, nodded in agreement to the proposed solutions, and promised to practice their English more. Predictably, none of the "agreements" made at the meeting worked, which further frustrated the Americans.

Upon examining this process later, it became obvious why it failed. Although the human resources managers were skilled facilitators of conflict resolution meetings, most of their experience was with groups composed solely of Americans. Their assumptions about how to effectively motivate participants to become involved in the process of such a meeting were based on the American model, which presumed that the Japanese would be comfortable with public disclosure and assert themselves in the context of a large group. In fact, they were not, these behaviors being quite foreign to general Japanese communication styles, especially in group meetings with non-Japanese. The Americans would have been much more successful conducting the meetings with the Japanese one-on-one. An even more effective approach would have been to use a Japanese manager to conduct the interviews. Interviews conducted in Japanese by a manager they knew and trusted would have helped the Japanese relax and would have resulted in much richer material. The group meeting was ineffective because the facilitators were blind to the need of the Japanese to discuss sensitive matters in private and come to a decision before making a public statement or announcement. Another effective approach would have been to form small monocultural groups of Americans and Japanese, ask each group to answer a set of questions provided by the facilitators, and then reconvene and report their findings. This approach can be used effectively in the conflict resolution process, even when only Americans are involved, but it is essential when Japanese are on one side of the conflict. More effort is needed to help the

Japanese open up and disclose sensitive information. We will note in the seven-step model where the use of monocultural groups can be most effective.

Here, briefly, is the substance of what each step in the seven-step model covers along with—in the first five steps— specific methodologies (the "facilitation strategies" mentioned above) that can be implemented by trainers, facilitators, and HR personnel in the conflict resolution process.

Step 1
Problem Identification

We initially present an organizational problem rising out of a cultural conflict as perceived by both Japanese and Americans. The problem represents a normal event which often occurs in U.S.-based Japanese companies and which critically affects organizational operations.

A. Statement of the Problem

First is a brief statement of the problem and its background. Often people see the same event from different perspectives. If they can first come to an agreement as to what the problem is, that shared perception will give them an advantage in attempting to solve it.

B. Description of the Incident

Next comes a brief description of a situation or incident that has actually occurred in a U.S.-based Japanese subsidiary from both the Japanese and American viewpoints. This format will reveal why reaching a consensus on a description of the incident is sometimes a difficult task.

Facilitation Strategies

In monocultural groups, do the following:

A. Identify the common or typical approach to dealing with this kind of problem in one's own culture.

B. Describe the problem experienced as a result of differences in the way Japanese and Americans approach the issue in question.

C. Have the Americans develop (from their perspective) for the Japanese group a full explanation of how and why this difficulty is occurring.

D. Have the Japanese develop (from their perspective) a full explanation for the American group of how and why this difficulty is occurring.

> *Note*: This step in the resolution model is a very important one, but it is often ignored. It is critical for each group, independent of the other, to have the opportunity to air its grievances about each other. When facilitated properly, there are a number of benefits to sharing information in a monocultural group at this stage in the process.

1. Participants go through an emotion-releasing, sometimes even cathartic experience which can prepare them for further learning.

2. Participants recognize that they are not alone in experiencing the conflict, that is, it is not abnormal.

3. Participants can explore strategies for cross-cultural interaction which they have individually found effective in the past.

4. Participants can generate useful, data-based feedback for presentation to the other culture group.

5. Participants may find a diversity in their perceptions of the incident that suggests their reaction may be more personal than they thought.

Step 2
Problem Clarification

Here the intentions of each side—that is, the Japanese and Americans involved in the event—are compared with the perception the other side has of them, throwing light on the nature of the misunderstanding. Because the discordance between intentions and perceptions is a frequent cause of conflict, it is necessary to clarify the intentions and perceptions in order to get at the root of a problem.

A. Comparative Intentions

An understanding of what the Japanese and Americans intended by their individual actions is necessary. Note that the intentions are normally felt as positive by the actors but are often perceived as negative by members of the other culture.

B. Comparative Perceptions

Perceptions of "what really happened" often vary according to culture. Likewise, interpretations and judgments about the other person's behavior depend significantly on culturally influenced expectations and assumptions.

Facilitation Strategies

A. Have the Americans explain and clarify to the Japanese the common or typical approaches to and strategies used in dealing with this kind of problem in the United States. It is especially important to clarify the logic or rationale and the feeling or emotion behind the approaches and strategies.

B. Then let the Japanese explain and clarify to the Americans the common or typical approaches and strategies used in Japan. Again, it is important to clarify the logic or rationale and the feelings or emotion behind their approaches and strategies.

C. Ask the American and Japanese participants to rejoin their monocultural groups and adjourn to separate rooms to discuss their reactions amongst themselves.

D. Reconvene and let each group discuss the outcome of its meeting with the other group.

E. Based upon the logic identified in steps A and B, help the Japanese and Americans reach a mutual understanding (not necessarily acceptance) of each other's approach. This step reinforces the idea that within every culture there are reasonable explanations for any given behavior and underlines the importance of each side recognizing that fact.

> *Note:* This process is an effective way to foster in the minds of people from one culture a more accurate understanding of another culture and to begin validating differences in their approaches to business and workplace issues.

Step 3
Cultural Exploration

This step examines the values of each culture and how they play out in light of contrasting expectations and assumptions. These expectations and assumptions drive the intentions and perceptions discussed in step 2.

A. Hidden Cultural Expectations

"I wish they were more like us" and "Why don't they do it our (the right) way?" are commonly heard statements. This step examines how each group thinks the other should act, according to what that group believes is normal in such situations.

B. Hidden Cultural Assumptions and Values

This step focuses on how values affect the intentions of each group and the perceptions each has of the other. It also helps those involved take a deeper look at the origins and assumptions behind culturally determined behaviors and discover that "common sense" is often different in each culture.

Facilitation Strategies

In the bicultural group, explore and discuss the significance of the differences in approach, while also attending to the differences in communication style. In particular, examine how each group might feel practicing the other's approach, how easy or difficult it would be. Specifically, what emotional adjustments need to be made and what behavioral skills need to be acquired to enable each person to function effectively using the other group's approach.

> *Note:* An effective way of achieving this goal is to use a reverse role-play methodology. In essence, this requires the Japanese to participate in preselected role-play scenarios, using behavior common to the American group members. Similarly, it requires Americans to participate in preselected role-play scenarios using behavior common to the Japanese group members. As an example, under the topic of communication style, a Japanese participant might be asked to assume a more aggressive or interactive American style in a bicultural meeting. In contrast, an American participant might be asked to assume a more passive interactive Japanese style in the same meeting (which requires more reliance on non-verbal communication skills). These scenarios can be videotaped, then analyzed afterward to reinforce the learning of new skills.

Step 4
Organizational Exploration

This step takes a look at the organizational issues which have an impact on the conflict under discussion. Organizational characteristics often impose unexpressed standards, expectations, and values which affect how people work together. Each of these factors is a reflection of the culture of the organization at either the global (headquarters) or the local (subsidiary) level. The importance of this step lies in the degree to which each side in a conflict tends to be unaware of the organizational pressures being placed on the other side. Often, too little time is taken for the education of each in the organizational context of the other. In each of the following chapters, depending on whether the conflict is felt initially by the Japanese or the Americans, we approach the topic of organizational exploration at either the global or the local level first.

A. Global Imperatives

This step focuses on the hidden imposition of organizational expectations from headquarters, which is what the Japanese manager represents. These organizational imperatives are driven by the eight characteristics of organizations mentioned earlier: corporate values, business strategies, corporate structure, staffing policies, performance standards, operational systems, job skills, and professional style; and they are imbedded in the headquarters corporate culture. In order for the subsidiary to operate effectively as a part of the larger structure, these organizational imperatives must be taken into consideration.

Facilitation Strategies

Guide the participants in the conflict in examining the differences between the corporate cultures of headquarters in Japan and the U.S. subsidiary. The following questions are suggested: What is the corporate culture of the organization in Japan? What is the corporate culture of the organization in the U.S. subsidiary? What is the preferred way of managing the issue, and does this way support and manifest the core values of the organization? Why does headquarters expect a certain approach to resolving the issue? With this approach, are the needs of the American employees/customers being met? Are any of the values identified in either steps 1 (identify) or 2 (clarify) held in common by both Japanese and American managers?

> *Note:* This approach can be reinforced by a standard-setting exercise. Take the information gathered in the first four steps and challenge the participants to analyze the effectiveness of the current organization. It is important to do this from the perspective of both employees and customers. In this step, ask the Japanese and American managers to determine how to best utilize the unique qualities of their cultures. This requires that they decide where to combine, compromise, or synergize certain elements of the two cultures.

B. Local Conditions

This step focuses on the varying factors in the local workplace which affect the ability of the company to be competitive in the chosen marketplace. Certain organizational characteristics (corporate values, business strategies, corporate structure, staff characteristics, performance standards, operational systems, job skills, and professional style) must be carefully examined and understood with respect to the requirements of the local environment. Often, the Japanese managers sent out by headquarters are told very little about the structure of their industry in the United States or the nature of the local American workplace. This may be because they assume that the differences from those of the home culture are insignificant.

Facilitation Strategies

Ask the entire group to consider these questions: How do the laws of the state or of the U.S. government affect the approach? Are there industry-specific or labor-directed standards which must be adhered to? What are the standards of competitors in the United States? What are the expectations of American customers regarding products and service? What benchmarks are available which may suggest alternative approaches to creating a competitive edge?

> *Note:* This step gives the bicultural facilitation team valuable data which is useful when making recommendations to management in the United States and Japan. For example, is there strong union representation for hourly wage earners in the area? How sophisticated is the workforce; have many worked for other large corporations, or have they worked for smaller companies? Information on laws, compensation/benefits, and other employee expectations can be obtained from any number of sources.

Step 5
Conflict Resolution

This part of the process model emerges from the answers to two questions: What is the goal? and How do we attain it?

What Is the Goal?

A. Achieving Harmony

By identifying and clarifying the problem (steps 1 and 2), those in conflict arrive at a more thorough understanding of the incident and of the intentions they have *toward* and the perceptions they have *of* each other. By exploring hidden cultural expectations and assumptions and by becoming aware of the major global imperatives and critical local conditions involved (steps 3 and 4), they comprehend better the cultural and organizational framework in which the conflict is taking place. Only when all of these factors are understood and addressed are the parties ready to commit to the harmony needed to solve the problem together.

Since harmony in human relationships is the ultimate goal (at least in Japanese culture), until this goal is desired, those in conflict cannot work effectively together to set goals and seek solutions. A frequent cause of continued disharmony occurs when one manager (usually the higher-ranking member) assumes the role of bystander or observer. Instead of recognizing his or her part in the problem, the person in the observer role will too often accuse the other of bad intentions rather than seeing that he or she (the observer) is manifesting the very cross-cultural characteristics which are the source of the problem, for example, attribution of blame to the other.

Facilitation Strategies

One of the first steps in achieving harmony is determining and clarifying the perceived impact of the conflict on three corporate functions: business operations, customer service, and employee development. This is dealt with in the Key Issue Worksheet (page 31), where the key issue in the conflict is defined in a succinct statement and participants are asked to fill in the three blanks under "impact" relative to how they see the conflict affecting the three corporate functions listed above. In discussing these consequences of the conflict, the participants see more sharply the necessity of establishing a harmonious relationship, so they can work together to resolve it.

The members of the group need to take four critical steps in order to generate a context in which they can work harmoniously together. Readiness to take these steps will result from having worked through steps 1-4 of the model, examining the conflict from Japanese and American perspectives, as well as from global and local perspectives:

1. Each participant needs to be able to take responsibility for or "own" the problem.

2. Each must recognize that his or her perception of the action of the other does not necessarily coincide with what the *intention* of the other was.

3. Each must understand and accept as valid the cultural assumptions and expectations of the other culture and the differences between local and global perspectives which are central to the conflict.

4. With the spirit of harmony generated by taking these steps, the group members should collectively be able to commit themselves to working together toward resolution.

B. Goal Setting

Here, the participants in the conflict engage in a process designed to produce a shared goal. Beginning with a discussion of possible goals which are so abstract that agreement can be readily obtained, they work with each other on more and more concrete definitions of the overall goal. They move from the abstraction of a shared goal—the universals upon which most people in the same business organization can agree—to the concrete indicators of a successful achievement of that goal. In so doing, they build a shared definition of their goal. If the goal which emerges from this process is not shared by both parties, no real progress will be made toward a solution of the problem. The real differences in goals often reflect fundamental value differences, such as attitudes toward time (the American orientation toward short-term goals versus the Japanese commitment to long-term goals, for instance), or differences in the perceived priority of stakeholders. (Americans put shareholders first, which means a dynamic focus on the bottom line; the Japanese put customers first, which means demanding focus on quality and service. Their shareholders have been, in the past, comparatively content with lower profit margins than most American shareholders would accept.)

Facilitation Strategies

Given the collaborative effort required to develop a mutually acceptable goal statement, an effective facilitator is essential to the process. A single facilitator may sometimes work out if the person has a strongly bicultural background and can consider the issues objectively, but a team of two bicultural facilitators is better. In fact, the facilitator or mediator role is so important that we recommend it be filled by a team of one Japanese and one American, one of whom has highly developed mediation skills. We will expound on the importance of this elsewhere. But the critical point here is that two facilitators assure cultural equity in the discussion more readily than one, especially if that one is either Japanese or American. Ultimately, a mutually acceptable goal statement can serve as a foundation for addressing other problem areas.

> *Note:* This approach uses a consensus model and is a culmination of the procedures which have taken place in the previous steps. This is a critical point; first, because attaining consensus verifies that harmony has been achieved, and second, because the Japanese and American managers are required to commit to a direction in the form of a company or departmental goal which has the broadest possible support. But the goal must be achievable. If it is obviously just an idealistic statement, the risk is high that employees will ignore it. On the other hand, a visionary element in an achievable goal statement can increase motivation among the employees. Arriving at agreement on the goal statement is a challenge for the managers and facilitators alike. Since creating a successful goal statement relies upon broad

support from management in order to succeed, the decision-making process used in both establishing and pursuing the goal must accommodate the cultural needs (the styles of communicating, patterns of thinking, and ways of behaving) of both groups in order to achieve consensus. Instead of emphasizing unanimous verbal or written agreement, the consensus model recommended is one that stresses the importance of everyone being heard, attended to, and cared for so that each person feels included in and buys into the decision to move forward. This process, in fact, is precisely what the Japanese refer to when they use the word *consensus*.

How Do We Attain the Goal?

C. Strategic Transition Planning

Once those in the conflict produce a shared goal and concrete, measurable indications of its achievement, they must decide on a strategy for moving the organization from its present state to the state embodied in the goal. The decision whether to "build" or to "buy," for instance, often produces conflicts because of cultural differences in regard to issues of values around timing, cost, growth, employee development, and relationships. Effective transition planning can be facilitated with an identification of the current impediments to goal achievement and of the resources required from the local organization and the global or regional headquarters (as is done in chapter 4, "Business Strategies: Training and Development").

Facilitation Strategy

Use this opportunity to analyze the gaps between the goal statement and the current position of the organization on the issue. Identifying the conditions required for the goal to be achieved and the measurable indicators that it has been reached will help build an understanding of the gaps. Develop a list of impediments or barriers to and the resources required (e.g., financial, human, facilities, materials, etc.) for achieving the goals so as to identify the current status. Refer to the Key Issue Worksheet (page 31) to see how this strategy is integrated with the larger process of analyzing the conflict. This methodology will also contribute to the next step of action planning. When the gap is clearly articulated, the action planning steps will become clear.

D. Action Planning and Implementation

At this point, the participants translate the strategic plan into concrete steps involving who, what, where, when, and how. Once these specific questions are resolved, implementation can begin. It is important to note, however, that making these sorts of detailed decisions frequently involves a great deal of culturally based disagreement. Americans and Japanese often have very different assumptions regarding how to go about planning specific actions. One major difference to facilitate is the orientation toward individual assignments (American) and teamwork or task group assignments (Japanese).

Facilitation Strategy

Use the Key Issue Worksheet on page 31 to facilitate the group's action planning and implementation tactics and to build upon the previous gap analysis. Guide the group (1) in identifying the gaps between the goal statement and current status, (2) in finding resources to surmount those barriers, and (3) in developing measurable indicators of achievement of the goal. They will have many ideas which may be misjudged across cultures, so remain focused on the processes in steps 1 through 4 of the worksheet in order to work through misunderstandings that occur en route. Don't hesitate to check intentions, perceptions, assumptions, and expectations of local subsidiary and global/regional headquarters as they are implied in members' discussions. First ask the individuals to fill out worksheets (or if the Japanese aren't ready to participate individually, begin with small-group worksheets), then do total, bicultural group worksheets. When the large or total group worksheet is completed with consensus, the action steps are ready for implementation. Ideally, the strengths of each member of the group have been applied to the discussion, and all commit to the group's achievement of the goal.

Key Issue Worksheet

1. Key Issue:		
2. Current Status and Impact on:		
a. Operations	b. Customers	c. Employees (and HQ, if applicable)
3. Goal Statement:		
4. Key Benefits to:		
a. Operational Excellence	b. Quality of Service to Customers	c. Development of Employees
5. Barriers to Change:		
6. Sources of Support:		
a. Internal	b. External	
7. Action Plan:		
a. Responsibility	b. Target Dates	
8. Success Factors:		

These dimensions of step five are often most effectively pursued through the use of a key issue analysis, which is facilitated by the Key Issue Worksheet above. The Key Issue Worksheet is usually introduced as the core focus of an off-site workshop for the Japanese and Americans engaged in the conflict situation. It involves

1. identifying the *key issue*. This will have been done in the first four steps (of the seven-step process) and simply needs to be clearly stated in a manner that incorporates the positive intent of each side in the conflict.

2. describing the *current status*, that is, the impact of the conflict on the operations, customers, and employees. If the resolution is going to have a significant impact on headquarters, then that should be included as a fourth domain.

3. developing a *goal statement* which is broadly conceived and that both sides can agree on, yet sufficiently refined and concrete to serve as an effective guide and motivation to action. This is the most difficult step in using the Key Issue Worksheet.

4. outlining the *key benefits* that will follow from achieving the stated goals. These fall into the three domains discussed under current status, that is, the benefits will be in the areas experiencing the greatest impact of the conflict identified in the key issue. Examining the key benefits may be of help in coming up with the final articulation of the goals.

5. identifying *barriers to change* within a functional context, that is, describing the obstacles (to achieving the goals) in concrete terms, for example, budget limitations, unavailability of specific skills, lack of information, and so forth, rather than simply blaming individuals or corporate divisions. In other words, be specific.

6. listing the *sources of support* available in confronting the barriers, such as external training, unexploited skills, and sources of or substitutes for needed funding.

7. developing an *action plan* for surmounting the barriers and achieving the goals. Outline and sequence the steps with attention to transition planning from one step to the next, that is, who does what when.

8. noting the *success factors* which signal progress. This means drawing up guidelines for monitoring success in achieving the goals and then publicizing the attainment of each milestone.

Step 6
Impact Assessment

This step clarifies the means of measuring the key indicators of success, which will determine the achievement of the goal and the group's resolution of the conflict. Because the two cultures often have different assumptions about what success is, these indicators will have been, one hopes, agreed upon by consensus in the same way that the goals in the previous step were. If the impact of the solution is not carefully and systematically assessed, the organization will have no way of knowing whether the root problem which resulted in the conflict has been solved. If no assessment is performed, there can even be uncertainty about whether the strategic plan was ever implemented. We have often seen the hopes of enthusiastic subsidiary employees dashed when their constructive suggestions for resolution receive no response from top management at headquarters or their representatives in the United States. Mutually agreed-upon assessment procedures will assure all parties of the seriousness of the group's work and will reflect a higher quality of relationships across cultures.

A. Monitoring Results

This step involves using the necessary tools and placing the responsible individuals in a position to assess achievements along established time lines in order to monitor progress.

During the action planning stage, a system for monitoring results needs to be established in order to clarify

- who has responsibility for checking progress,
- what device will be used to monitor progress, and
- when the monitoring will be done.

Monitoring results at different stages is an important part of motivating the workforce. If workers are not told until the end whether or not success has been achieved, they will not be motivated to make an effort to ensure that it is.

B. Modifying the Plan

The purpose of frequent assessment is to modify the action plan if it is not achieving the desired results along the appropriate time line. This section in each of the following eight chapters examines whether the implementation of the action plan is succeeding and directs the participants to modify their action plan if problems are occurring.

C. Assessing Benefits

After the ultimate goal is achieved, it is important to determine the ways in which the organization changed as a result of achieving the goal. What specifically was the benefit to the organization—both at headquarters and in the subsidiary—which followed the achievement of this goal? The most important one is a reduction of conflict and an increase in morale, which causes productivity to increase. Another benefit may be a decline in absenteeism or employee turnover. In addition, it would be a significant accomplishment if the negative impacts of the conflict on the three critical parties (employees, customers, and business) identified in the worksheet had been turned around. These accomplishments could be measured in terms of the positive consequences the conflict resolution had brought about in these three areas.

Step 7
Organizational Integration

This step takes the results of the conflict resolution and assessment data and distributes them throughout the company, integrating individual success stories into corporate learning systems. Conflict and its resolution may occur in a single department without people in other departments hearing about it. Through integration, the entire company can benefit from the process and the results. At the same time, the individuals involved in the original conflict are given an opportunity to integrate the key learnings of the conflict resolution process into their own personal working styles and, perhaps, be celebrated for their creative contributions.

A. Recording Results

In this section, the entire process—the problem as it was, how it was approached, and how it was resolved—is entered into the documentation of the company (e.g., as a feature story in the internal newsletter or as a distributed case study report) so that the path of development is clear to those who follow. Recording results eliminates the perception that the problem was resolved haphazardly and provides information helpful in determining accountability, reward systems, and models for future conflict resolution.

B. Celebrating Achievements

This step focuses on drawing the group's attention to the achievement of results by pausing, reflecting, and celebrating in a group context (e.g., a departmental dinner, a team excursion, or a special staff meeting). Such celebrations are part of the intrinsic reward system—they give solidarity, build teamwork, and create role models.

C. Institutionalizing Benefits

To perpetuate the accrual of benefits to the organization by achieving results in this conflict resolution model, the company can work to take the key learnings which resulted from the process and apply them elsewhere in the organization. In so doing other similar conflicts can be avoided. The resolution of one conflict can suggest changes which would be effective in resolving other conflicts which involve the same general issues. By integrating the key learnings of one department into the operating systems of the corporation as a whole, the organization can reduce the effort and energy which are wasted when culturally based misunderstandings occur. Actual competencies and skill sets which are learned by experiencing this process could be institutionalized in the training, evaluation, and reward systems across the company.

Our experience in dealing with U.S.-based Japanese subsidiaries has led us to believe that completing all seven steps of this conflict resolution process is crucial to the long-term success of managing cultural conflict. We realize, however, that some of the Japanese and Americans in the companies we have worked with merely want to know what their cultural counterpart is thinking. Armed with this knowledge, many Americans and Japanese have said they could at least survive the frustration they were feeling. They don't necessarily expect the behavior of the other person to change (indeed, many wish it not to). For those whose interest is limited to getting a better understanding of their cultural counterpart, we recommend they focus on the first four steps of the seven-step conflict resolution process: (1) problem identification, (2) problem clarification, (3) cultural exploration, and (4) organizational exploration.

For example, after completing these four steps toward harmony, many Americans are relieved to learn about the tendency of Japanese managers to give negative feedback to their subordinates as a strategy for motivation. We have heard the following from countless Americans:

> After I realized why my Japanese manager constantly criticized all of his subordinates, both Japanese and American, I felt greatly relieved. Until then, I was constantly worrying that I had done something wrong. Now that I know it is part of a fairly common Japanese management style, I don't take it personally. It's simply a Japanese management tool.

Americans who recognize this pattern of feedback realize that their Japanese managers are not biased against them. They also understand that their manager may never change and may continue to dole out primarily negative (and seldom positive) feedback. Nonetheless, that understanding alone can be extremely helpful in enabling them to adapt to a very foreign management style and enjoy a more harmonious workplace.

Part Two

Problem Areas

3

Corporate Values

Case Study: Work Habits

In considering the merging of two or more national or ethnic cultures in an organization which must work dynamically and smoothly, one of the most fundamental contrasting elements of culture is underlying values. Understanding the values of a culture involves understanding the foundations on which judgments and interpretations of what is good and right are made. The discovery that values about family, workplace, friends, and so on are not shared by both participants in a conflict compels us to work at creating an organizational environment where values are at worst seen as complementary and at best as extensively shared. When corporate values are not shared, conflicts—along with decreases in productivity and morale—are inevitable.

From an intercultural perspective, then, *corporate values* are the most fundamental, the most deeply hidden organizational characteristic that drives acceptable work habits. As a result, a difference in values is almost always involved in cultural conflicts within the organization. It is wise therefore to look for the cultural values involved in every such conflict. To understand conflicts involving work habits we need to dig down into the motivating values which cause people to behave as they do. Values strongly influence our judgment of right and wrong. The development of assumptions about the rightness or wrongness of particular work habits is no exception. When value-driven assumptions about work habits clash, the result can be a very emotional and seemingly intractable conflict, such as the one we are about to describe.

Step 1
Problem Identification

A. Statement of the Problem

"When the going gets tough, Americans tend to switch companies." Many Japanese look at the high rate of attrition among American upper- and middle-level managers with a combination of amusement and disgust. "How can we grow to trust them if we know that it is only a matter of time before they are gone?" one Japanese asked. It is even more amazing to the Japanese when an American is rehired by a company he or she previously left. "Where is the loyalty?" Americans, on the other hand, feel that the well-known loyalty of the Japanese represents a lack of choices. "The Japanese are nothing more than indentured servants because they have no option to leave and be hired by a different company."

The idea of reducing work hours—hours that Americans see as excessive but Japanese view as necessary due partly to the extreme loyalty demanded of them—has been a highly publicized and emotional topic in recent years among the Japanese. Many corporations and government offices have instituted various strategies to accomplish this reduction.

Everything from mandatory "leave early" days to increasing the number of company and personal health holidays has been tried. The idea of balancing one's personal and professional lives is an especially hot topic among younger Japanese professionals. The so-called *Shin-Jin-Rui*, or new generation, seems no longer willing to put up with the sacrifices made by their predecessors. They realize that the economy in Japan is much tighter than in the past and fewer companies are offering the so-called lifetime employment guarantees. In fact, an increasing number of Japanese companies are now basing salary increases and promotions more on performance than ever before. This is a huge departure from the traditional method of considering seniority or amount of time at current level when handing out raises or promotions. The environment in Japan is changing, and younger employees are not as willing as their predecessors to sacrifice personal gain or comfort for the good of the company. Nonetheless, in spite of the changes in Japan, as a result of the economy and the attitude of the *Shin-Jin-Rui,* the effect on the Japanese companies in the United States has been minimal. American workers still feel that their Japanese managers expect them to spend too much time on the job and to put the good of the company over individual (selfish, as perceived by the Japanese) needs. This is because most Japanese expatriate managers in the United States are older than most members of the *Shin-Jin-Rui* generation. They still have the more conservative attitudes of the "older generation" and tend to hold dearly to those attitudes even in the United States. In fact, it is not uncommon for younger Japanese (mid-20s to early 30s) to have much better relationships with their American counterparts than with Japanese. Of course, most of these younger Japanese have no American subordinates; their relationships with Americans are as colleagues with no reporting structure at all.

These widely divergent attitudes regarding daily work practices make for a significant problem in many U.S.-based Japanese companies. There are really two questions involved in these conflicts. First, how much time should a worker spend on the job? Americans and Japanese tend to disagree on what constitutes a fair day's work for a fair day's pay and on whether there is always a relationship between the number of hours spent at the company and the number of tasks accomplished. Second, should workers place their loyalty primarily with the company or with their families and/or individual career goals? Japanese tend to be loyal to the company, while Americans place more emphasis on their families. However, the Japanese view working long hours to achieve success at one's job as the correct way to demonstrate love for one's family, while Americans emphasize spending "quality time" at home. These differences in attitude can generate a great deal of resentment among Americans and Japanese working together. Americans regard Japanese who continually work late into the night, sacrificing time with their families, as foolish. The Japanese view Americans who refuse to spend time working late as selfishly sacrificing the company on the altar of their personal time and family needs.

B. Description of the Incident

A Japanese manager in charge of a production department for a parts supplier was faced with a recurring problem in his area. One part consistently had the same defect. He and his American subordinates had been working on solving the problem for several weeks, but little progress had been made. Not sensing an imminent solution, he mandated that his staff of seven employees, all of whom were part of the salaried American management team, participate in a series of task force meetings to solve the problem. The meetings would be held daily, Monday through Friday, would run from 7:00-8:00 P.M., and would continue until the problem was solved. Upon hearing this, the Americans were indignant. They were used to working long hours, depending on the severity of the problem, but being required to attend the new meetings would mean working at least twelve hours every day of the workweek. Reluctantly, they agreed to participate. Within three weeks, the morale of the whole department had deteriorated considerably.

Japanese Perspective

The Japanese manager was confused by the attitudes of his staff.

> I don't see why they are complaining. I work at least thirteen or fourteen hours a day, so I'm not asking them to do anything I wouldn't do. We have a severe problem to take care of, and all they can think about is getting home early enough to mow their lawns or play tennis. They are always taking from the company and never giving back.

American Perspective

The Americans, on the other hand, started to think of their Japanese supervisor as a "slave driver." They felt that the new meetings were unreasonable. "Our Japanese manager has always placed more emphasis on how late we work than on what we get done," one worker said.

> Now, with this 7:00 P.M. meeting, he is just trying to assert his authority over us. Besides, we haven't accomplished any more in the meetings than we do in our regular interactions throughout the day. He wants us to stay late so he'll look good to his Japanese boss, even though we aren't any closer to solving the problem now than we were before. We have lives outside of this company, and we resent the pressure he puts on us to stay late, especially on Friday evenings, since that is essentially part of the weekend. His plan cuts into our personal time too much. Maybe the Japanese don't care about their families, but we have spouses and children whom we would like to see more often than on the weekends.

Step 2
Problem Clarification

Intentions versus Perceptions

Intentions	
Japanese	**American**
• Solve the problem • Demonstrate commitment to the company	• Work hard during normal hours • Maintain the integrity of their private lives

Perceptions	
Japanese	**American**
• The workers are being selfish • The workers complain too much	• The supervisor does not appreciate our effort • The supervisor does not take our needs into consideration

Japanese Perspective

By ordering the task force meetings, the Japanese manager intended to solve the problem and to demonstrate his department's commitment to the company. "My staff needs to know that we have a lot of pressure to perform well," he explained.

> Our productivity is constantly being compared to that of other operations around the world, and we must strive to improve continuously. By all of us participating in a daily meeting which starts at 7:00 P.M., we are showing our management and our customers that we are making every effort to improve.

From his perspective, the American workers were deficient in being unable to place the good of the company before their own selfish desires. "I wish my staff would work like the Japanese engineers and do their jobs without complaining."

American Perspective

In reacting to their supervisor's new schedule of evening meetings, the American workers focused on the fact that they worked hard during normal business hours and preferred not to sacrifice their private lives by working overtime unnecessarily. "We realize that a lot of work needs to be done to solve this problem," one American said. "However, it is only one of many issues that we have to deal with every day. Our job is never completed, so it is quite difficult to decide on a fair quitting time. In any event, what we don't finish today will always be waiting for us tomorrow." From their perspective, their supervisor was failing to appreciate their sacrifices.

> What really bothers us is that he never thanks us for all the extra effort we already put in. Although we regularly work late and even come in on weekends to take care of emergencies, he never gives us a pat on the back or tells us to take a half day off as comp time for the hard work. We were already feeling taken for granted, and when he ordered us to participate in the 7:00 P.M. meetings, where he did nothing but criticize us, it was the last straw. It would be nice if he operated on our schedule and in our style once in a while.

Step 3
Cultural Exploration

Expectations and Assumptions	
Japanese	**American**
Appreciation shown for hard work	
• Employees should sacrifice and work hard for the benefit of the group • Working long hours is an appropriate demonstration of effort and commitment	• Employees should have control over their own lives and have a right to private time • Working effectively is more important than working long hours

Japanese Perspective

Japanese value self-sacrifice and place a high priority on working hard for the benefit of the group. "The group" can be represented by a task team, a product division, or the company as a whole. As a member of the group, there is great peer pressure to conform to its needs. It is expected that one will sacrifice almost anything related to personal comfort or immediate satisfaction in order to promote success or otherwise fulfill the needs of the group. As a result, the Japanese spend a great deal of time and energy showing others that they are working very hard for the good of the group while sacrificing their own personal needs. This exhibition of effort—*doryoku*—is highly valued among the Japanese. There are many ways to exhibit *doryoku:*

- Remaining in the office later than one's manager

- Not complaining about the conditions of the workplace (that it is too hot or cold, or that the uniforms do not fit)

- Dragging oneself into the office immediately after returning from an overseas business trip, even though experiencing jet lag to the point of being unable to get any work done

- Working late into the night on a regular basis
- Accomplishing tasks at great personal cost or sacrifice

Obviously, the Japanese manager in this case was upset that his American workers were not exhibiting *doryoku*.

Many of the values surrounding the Japanese notions of self-sacrifice, discipline, loyalty to one's "master," group identity, and commitment to the group can be traced to religious and philosophical influences. It is not the purpose of this book to provide an exhaustive study of these influences, but it is important to note that Confucianism, Buddhism, and Shinto have all contributed to the development of the values of the Japanese culture in these matters. Confucianism brought with it a status-conscious awareness of and emphasis on hierarchically arranged roles in society. In the Confucian system of thought, one's role determines the rules of behavior to which one is expected to adhere. One consequence of the Buddhist tradition in Japan has been to place great value on other-centeredness and self-denial. One effect of this has been to emphasize the value of relationships over the value of the individual. The essence of the Shinto religion is harmony—harmony manifested by the right relations and balance between gods and nature (including humans)—and the harmonious relationship of self to other. Harmony perpetuates the Shinto faith, while a lack of harmony is seen as the essence of immorality.

American Perspective

There are two main reasons for the resentment which developed among the Americans in this situation. First, the Americans were upset by the lack of flexibility or freedom. Second, they felt that their supervisor did not demonstrate an understanding of the nature of hard work. Americans believe that hard work involves working effectively with good time management skills, as opposed to working long hours to show you can work as hard and sacrifice as much as others in the company. When the Japanese manager mandated that the meetings start at a time considered late by most Americans, he was violating the American reverence for time management. Time management reflects the value Americans place on having a sense of control over their lives, which suits them as independent, self-reliant individuals. Time management training seminars have been conducted in virtually every city in the United States and at most large American corporations. Americans pride themselves on working fast and efficiently. Since many jobs are structured to be handled individually, people in management positions can exert a great deal of control over their own schedules. Unfortunately, this can mean overlooking details or putting off completing a job until the next day, when, by merely staying late, one could finish it. On the other hand, many Americans who follow events in Japan are intrigued by the phenomenon of *karoshi* (death from being overworked) but argue that no job is worth that great a sacrifice.

Step 4
Organizational Exploration

Global Imperatives   Local Conditions

Japanese	American
• Group work is key—the whole group works together to solve the problem • Headquarters must be confident we can do the job	• The interest of the individual worker must be balanced with the needs of the group and company

Japanese Perspective (Global Imperatives)

The Japanese manager in this case was operating under the influence of several global imperatives. He shared the organizational values held by company headquarters in Japan, which involved the pursuit of perfection, that is, the production of a perfect product, the satisfaction of his customers, and the demonstration of effort on the part of his workers. One of his most basic values was the importance of group work. In his value system, one person was not expected to stay behind and finish—the whole group was expected to stay, even if not all of them were working productively. To him this was common sense, natural behavior. These values are common in the Japanese manufacturing sector and were particularly strong in the company in question. From the perspective of the headquarters organization in Japan, the greatest perfection of product development was accomplished when the team was totally operable; individuals were to subjugate their personal needs to the good of the team. In mandating a series of late staff meetings to solve a recurring problem, the Japanese manager was simply responding in the most logical way for someone whose values were in line with the parent company in Japan.

Equally important is the Japanese belief, in direct opposition to the American, that much more time than a five-day week of eight-hour days is needed to deal with everything that occurs in a Japanese company. Given the indirectness and complexity of the Japanese communication style, their need to maintain harmonious relations, and the value employees place on positive relations with their bosses and coworkers, it is not surprising that they see logic in the greater demands placed upon their time, which results in work days stretching far into the evening.

It is not simply the slow pace of the process and the Japanese need to stretch out workplace interaction that calls for more job time among the Japanese, nor are the Japanese obsessed with accomplishing more in the fashion of true workaholics. The atmosphere in a Japanese corporation— where a great deal must be accomplished under heavy personal relations constraints (which we will explore in more detail later in this book)—produces a high degree of individual stress, which finds its release in the evenings they spend drinking together. This is a global imperative for Japanese working anywhere in the Japanese corporate system.

American Perspective (Local Conditions)

The American workers, on the other hand, were being influenced by values imposed upon them by local conditions. The limitations on the workday in American industry were won by labor unions in hard-fought battles between labor and management and are seen to protect the interests of the individual worker at all levels. Even though the employees involved in this incident were primarily salaried and not hourly workers, the feeling of a fair day's work for a fair day's pay was still strong. Observance of important national holidays is another privilege brought about in part through the efforts of American labor unions, and this extends to weekends as well. The labor movement is proud of having won concessions from management, and managers who try to take away workers' personal privileges are seen as representative of the sort of people who forced the unions to form in the first place. Americans feel that the question, Can workers achieve enough in an eight-hour day to justify the money they receive? was answered long ago. By protesting the Japanese manager's decision to extend working hours, the American workers, though in management positions themselves, were simply responding in the most logical way for people whose values were in line with the mainstream of the manufacturing sector in America.

It is important to remember that belief in the values described here or anywhere else in this book is neither uniform nor universal among Japanese or Americans. There are many Americans, of course, who just as regularly as the Japanese sacrifice time with their families or their own health for the company. Similarly there are increasing numbers of Japanese who see the old patterns of company loyalty as archaic and/or destructive. A key component in the frustration of the Americans in this case, however, was the way the Japanese mandated their participation in the meetings—violating their need to feel they have individual and independent control over their lives.

Step 5
Conflict Resolution

Disturbed by the decline in morale and the seemingly intractable nature of the conflict, the Japanese human resources manager, with the support of outside consultants, decided to attempt to act as mediator between the two sides. Assisted by the American associate human resources manager, the Japanese manager conducted an assessment of the problem, including interviews with a selected sample of participants on both sides of the conflict. The data they collected formed the basis for the first four of our seven steps: (1) problem identification, (2) problem clarification, (3) cultural exploration, and (4) organizational exploration.

One thing that became clear in this process was the importance of different perceptions of family life. A major obstacle to achieving harmony in the situation was that neither the Japanese managers nor their American subordinates were familiar with each other's family lifestyles. This discovery followed directly from their data-gathering exercise and is a good example of effective problem clarification. It also led directly to useful cultural exploration. In an effort to lead by example, it was suggested that the senior American operations manager invite his Japanese supervisor, the plant manager, to a series of dinners which would allow him and the Japanese supervisor the opportunity to get to know each other better. Furthermore, after they were more comfortable with each other, they had the option of inviting each other to their homes for casual dinners. Even though the Japanese typically may not feel comfortable entertaining or being entertained in private residences, this would provide an opportunity to understand and experience what family life meant to each other.

It was quite successful. The American's wife and children got along well with their Japanese counterparts, and on several occasions the differences between American and Japanese family life were discussed, not only by the two men but also by their wives. For his part, the Japanese plant manager was impressed by the close relationship his American subordinate enjoyed with his family. The American operations manager, on the other hand, came to appreciate the high value his Japanese supervisor placed on family, despite the strong Japanese emphasis on company loyalty. The Japanese manager and his American subordinate agreed that they would use their common experiences and new understanding to help them and others on the management team resolve the conflict over work habits.

Shortly thereafter, the Japanese plant manager called a meeting of all the top managers—both Japanese and American—at the plant (not just those in the department where the conflict arose). He described the experience of having several dinners with the operations manager alone and some with his family. He explained that he had become aware of the importance and great value American families place on their evening time together. The American manager expressed his newfound appreciation for Japanese family values and explained how he had come to understand the differences between American and Japanese work schedules. Both men encouraged the teams of Americans and Japanese to take time during lunches and after work to get to know each other better and not just interact on the job. In this atmosphere further discussions took place aimed at the critical goal—developing a commonly held set of norms or standards which satisfies both Japanese and American expectations in regard to discipline, loyalty, effort, productivity, flexibility, and freedom. These work norms must be perceived as reasonable by both groups and can only be created by informed discussion among the parties involved based on respect. Having established the right atmosphere, the resolution of the conflict proceeded relatively smoothly.

Those in conflict were able to agree on a schedule of meetings at which to address their recurrent manufacturing problem. The important issue, of course, was to meet the needs of the Americans while assuring that no work time was lost. In the end, the Americans committed to a schedule which brought them into work early three days a week. In exchange, the Japanese agreed to move the task force meeting time from 7:00 P.M. to 5:00 P.M. so that the Americans could leave the office by 6:00 or 6:30. The Japanese also agreed to conduct Friday meetings in the morning from 7:00 to 8:30 rather than after work, allowing the Americans to spend that very important Friday evening with their families. With this arrangement, there was no conflict with the Japanese manager's effort to exhibit the proper amount of effort, *doryoku*, to his counterpart at headquarters. As far as the Friday schedule is concerned, because of the time difference between Japan and the United States, Friday evenings are actually Saturday afternoon in Japan, thus, the supervisor there was already gone; he did not work on Saturdays. This harmonious resolution of the conflict enhanced the appreciation of each group for the other and fostered feelings of mutual respect.

Step 6
Impact Assessment

As the new strategy and the new action plan were implemented, the human resources manager oversaw and assessed their progress in resolving the conflict. After several months, the Japanese manager conducted a survey of employee attitudes and discovered that much of the previous decline in morale had been reversed. Some minor modifications, including more specific guidelines, were made in the action plan for working hours. Ongoing productivity assessments determined that no significant decline in output had resulted from the new work schedule. Eventually, the recurrent defect problem was solved by the task force.

After a few more months, the human resources manager and plant manager were satisfied that the original goals had been met and that the action plan had succeeded in producing results. Morale was markedly higher, and the productivity and quality problems had been solved. There were, in addition, two side benefits to the organization which are worth noting. One was that the Japanese manager discovered a tactic for motivating his workers which many American managers use on a regular basis—a commitment to respect workers' private time as a reward for hard work. Another benefit to the organization was the development of a productive, integrated team. Instead of continuing to be at odds with their subordinates over work issues, the Japanese managers found it much easier to deal with the Americans whose teamwork improved under the new system. This emerging sense of teamwork was strengthened even further by the integration policies implemented by the company.

Step 7
Organizational Integration

The conflict in this case initially occurred among the members of a single team in the manufacturing plant. Yet the Japanese plant manager made certain that all of the department managers were involved in the initial goal-setting process. If the entire plant was to benefit from conflict resolving process they were putting in motion, then other departments would need to be involved in it as soon and as much as possible. The plant manager also attempted, even before the first meeting, to achieve some level of consensus among his Japanese subordinates in order to make sure that they were all in agreement with the new direction he planned to take.

Under the new system, managers had the right to request work beyond normal hours in order to solve emerging problems. Managers would, however, make a commitment to allow their American subordinates to go home by 6:30. After the assessment team had made its final report, the associate human resources manager wrote a draft of the new work rules in the employee handbook. Having already achieved the support of each department manager, the revisions were quickly approved.

By way of celebrating their achievements, the Japanese department managers organized a company party at the end of the year. There, a toast was offered by the American operations manager to the Japanese plant manager, thanking him for his appreciation and support of the Americans in maintaining a balance between their professional and personal lives. One Japanese department manager joined the operations manager in toasting their superior, thanking him in a characteristic Japanese fashion for his leadership in restoring harmony to the plant.

By including the full range of department managers in the entire conflict resolution process, the plant manager had already gone a long way toward institutionalizing the benefits gained by resolving the initial conflict. Because he had been so deeply influenced by his contact with the American operations manager's family, however, he made one additional suggestion; he encouraged all of his Japanese department managers to try the same sort of cultural exchange with their American subordinates. It soon became the practice of the top-ranking American in each department to go out to dinner with his or her Japanese manager at least once each month. Some of the Japanese and Americans pursued the approach of having private dinners at their homes with the families of their counterparts. In addition, holding an annual end-of-the-year party became a tradition at the plant.

Although the critical incident we have used to illustrate the potential conflicts surrounding work habits deals primarily with the question of reasonable working hours, there are many other work habits about which Japanese and Americans have differing opinions. Questions of timing and duration of lunch hours, punctuality, taking calls during meetings, smoking, and so on can generate conflicts which are just as serious as the one we have just described.

Business Strategies

Case Study: Training and Development

Culture influences every dynamic between human beings, and all *business strategies* are dependent upon the responses of the people involved. It is not surprising, therefore, that cultural conflicts can be created, escalated, lessened, or resolved by an organization's strategic decisions. Second to corporate values, business strategy is the one area where the contrasting elements of two cultures are most often played out by top management in multinational organizations. Determining effective business strategy requires an understanding of how management can engage, motivate, and develop human beings in a chosen direction. Analyzing strategic plans uncovers important, culturally based assumptions about employees' values and about how an organization's top management expects its employees to function and to be motivated. When business strategies are not based on common assumptions and expectations, the people involved will surely come into conflict while attempting to execute those strategies.

The field of human resource planning focuses on the strategic engagement of human beings in the operation of the business and on the strategy by which a company develops its workers to manage the business. A key strategic question in the field of international human resource planning is how to utilize, develop, and motivate the human resources which the company has employed around the world. Specifically, how does culture influence a company's strategy of investing in the development of human resources in its subsidiaries abroad? If a company bases its training and development strategy on assumptions which are common to both management and workers, the result is usually positive; management develops the workforce in a manner conducive to the long-term interests of the company, and the workers are highly motivated to do their jobs well. Motivation works to increase morale and productivity—it is the fundamental element in managing human beings. If, on the other hand, management bases its training and development strategies on culturally specific assumptions which are in conflict with those of the workforce, morale and productivity decline, and conflicts such as the one we are about to describe often erupt.

Step 1
Problem Identification

A. Statement of the Problem

Business organizations in the United States are expected to be concerned about human resource development and to provide a certain amount of training to their employees. U.S.-based Japanese companies are reluctant to follow this practice because of the high turnover they find in the American workplace. Therefore, management in some U.S.-based Japanese firms commits very little to the training and development of its

American personnel for fear of losing the investment when the workers leave. In American society people who are successful are referred to as outstanding. They are quite visible and are offered opportunities for advancement and career development from many sources, including those outside their companies. In Japanese culture the emphasis tends to be on standing *in* rather than standing *out;* a successful worker is one who can be in harmony with both peers and with the company philosophy. Americans, on the other hand, feel that the investment their employer makes in their training and development represents an important commitment and constitutes a strong motivator for them to remain in the company. If there is no investment, no opportunity for growth and development, American employees are likely to seek alternative employment. In many ways, this is a classic catch-22.

If a risk is required to bridge the gap in this case, Americans feel that their Japanese managers must be willing to take it. Many American companies experience high turnover rates, yet the better ones still invest a great deal in training and development. If it is to be assumed that the Japanese ought to do the same, then questions arise regarding how much and what type of training to provide. This chapter will deal with three issues: (1) the role of training and who is responsible for it, (2) the responsibility for directing an individual's career path and the timing of change, and (3) the style of training and who must adapt it to fit the situation when styles conflict.

B. Description of the Incident

American employees in a Silicon Valley Japanese company complained that they hadn't had any real training for over a year. The personnel department told them that the Japanese were reluctant to invest in their training and development because the company's turnover rate that year was so high. This lowered morale because the employees believed training and development was their right. Finally, some trainers from Japan came to the company and conducted a five-day training program for all salespeople. From the outset, the American workers were uncertain what was going on. First, the training did not concern sales but was aimed instead at helping the employees understand some of the benefits of the new product line—the type of information that production or marketing people should be given. The employees had the strange feeling that they were being prepared for some unknown lateral job change. They felt the Japanese had little to teach them about how to sell to Americans. They also thought the training was boring. The trainers' English was poor, and their presentation style was very lecture-oriented. The Japanese trainers were only able to tell them the sorts of things salespeople in Japan do, which they found irrelevant to selling in the United States. Further, the program was rigidly structured. In the role plays they were expected to follow the exact form demonstrated by the trainers, which didn't work with the Americans. The training effort was a flop. Finally, in an effort to placate their employees, the personnel department prepared to offer packaged programs bought from outside training firms. But now the employees turned resentful, because they weren't consulted as to the kinds of programs they needed or allowed to help design them in-house.

Japanese Perspective

From the Japanese manager's perspective, the American workers were demonstrating an unacceptable level of self-interest and disloyalty. "When the Americans join our company, we pay them well and we expect them to be loyal," he said.

> We intend to take care of them in a way which enables them to grow together as a team and to feel the strength of their unity through shared skills and common goals. However, it seems that Americans are strong-willed individuals, motivated by selfish desires for rapid career advancement. We can see that they make more money

through job rotation to different companies but it destroys the company spirit and the harmony of our workplace to have people coming and going all the time. We want to invest in our employees' training and development. However, it is very difficult to take such a risk when data show us that 30 to 40 percent of our employees will be gone after we train them. Why should they go to local colleges and universities for advanced training when we can provide that internally? That is what a good company should do, train their employees using more senior employees as role models. Also, they should have more respect for their trainers from Japan. These trainers are masters at the skills they are transferring to the Americans. We lose face with our management team in Japan when the trainers return with stories of their American trainees' disrespectful behavior. Such trainers will not want to return to the United States in the future. This also discourages us from sending American trainees to Japan for training and development—we cannot trust them to demonstrate appropriate and respectful behavior there.

American Perspective

"The Japanese think they have a problem investing in our training and development because of high turnover, but they don't understand that our competitors in this industry also have high turnover," one American said in his interview.

This is the nature of the business. If they wish to keep us, they have to invest in our training and development and help us pursue our best career options within the company. We don't mind some job rotation as long as the path is going upward, but when we feel there is no opportunity for advancement, we naturally begin looking for outside opportunities. They pay us well when we join the company, so of course we would like to stay on board, but as Americans we need to be personally involved in determining our training needs and the style in which we are trained, as well as determining the direction of our careers. The Japanese seem to want us to leave those decisions in their hands. That isn't likely to happen. We are motivated by engagement, challenge, opportunity, and by being involved in the information flow and the decision-making process when it affects our own lives. Take those things away, and we're out of here.

Another problem that rankled the American salesforce was that although the company had a program which allowed a reimbursement for courses taken at accredited colleges and universities, they felt pressure from the Japanese not to use it.

Step 2
Problem Clarification

Intentions versus Perceptions

Intentions	
Japanese	**American**
• Train workers in ways beneficial both to them and to the company • Give opportunities selectively and at a low cost, using internal sources; be a good role model	• Improve performance and career potential through training • Have input regarding amount and type of training

Perceptions	
Japanese	**American**
• The workers are selfish and disruptive • We are reluctant to train our workers because they refuse to stay in one place for long • We are the role models for the employees. It is a waste of time and money to attend off-site classroom-style training	• The managers don't care about us as individuals and won't give us an opportunity to plan the training with them • The company won't give us training because it doesn't plan to keep us for long • The Japanese won't allow us to use our educational reimbursement benefits; they are cheap and controlling

Japanese Perspective

The Japanese managers were concerned with training their employees in appropriate ways which were beneficial to both the individual employee and the company. They wanted to give training opportunities selectively, as required by the particular situation. They also wanted to keep training costs at a minimum by purchasing outside training programs. From their perspective, the Americans were selfish, disruptive, and insensitive to the needs of the company. "As managers, we expect our employees to behave appropriately, with respect for their supervisors and their trainers," one Japanese manager said.

> It is our job to continually assess the competencies and performance of each employee in light of the organization as a whole. We are responsible for job rotation and career development, but we do want to know each employee's expectations. Sometimes it is difficult to ask them because they are so demanding. Perhaps our timing is off for the

American worker, but we expect them to be satisfied in each position for three to five years. There is much to learn in each position, and much experience is required. We cannot make the rapid changes they expect.

American Perspective

In this situation, the American workers were trying to improve their own performance and career potential through training, and they wanted to have some input regarding the amount and type of training they received. From their perspective, their Japanese managers seemed not to care about them as individuals. They came to believe that the company would not invest in their development because it did not intend to allow them to keep their jobs for very long.

"They don't know American customers at all," one American worker complained. "They just got off the plane from Japan." The Americans wondered why the trainers didn't just present the information about the new product and let the salespeople take over from there. They told the personnel department that what they really needed was some training in supervisory or management skills in order to move up the career ladder and that they were not being given the time and resources that they deserved.

"In order to clarify our roles in this company," one distressed American explained,

> we need to sit down with our manager, just as we would in an American company, and talk about our expectations for training and development. Sometimes we do this with the director of personnel, who is American, but the personnel people are generally not included in strategic planning for human resources development, which is handled entirely by Japanese managers. The Japanese, therefore, never hear our opinions. If we could create a game plan together, knowing how

many hours a year we were to receive training, we would be highly motivated to stay with the company as long as we felt we were progressing along a career path as well—the two go hand in hand. We expect to be able to attend conferences, professional training seminars, or classes at the local university, but these opportunities are not made available to us by the Japanese managers. Also, we think the trainers who come from Japan should be taught how to work with Americans before they take charge of the training room. They don't have a clue as to how to deal with American trainees. Something so simple and obvious as respecting the trainee as a person and valuing his or her ideas and feelings is utterly beyond them.

Step 3
Cultural Exploration

Expectations and Assumptions

Japanese	American
• All workers are like beginners and can be trained without regard to individual variation	• Training should be targeted specifically to address workers' needs
• The company makes training decisions in order to assure equal opportunity	• Workers should be strategically involved in training decisions
• High turnover is unusual and leads to questions about workers' value to the company	• Training should be given regardless of turnover
• Good training involves providing a model for trainers to follow—trainers give feedback, but not vice versa	• Good training involves interaction with the trainer and individual attention

The strategy of investing in human resources through training and development is clearly important in both cultures. The amount of time that should be invested, however, and exactly how the training is conducted are questions to which each culture gives a different answer. In comparison to Japanese companies in Japan, American businesses do not invest a great deal of time in developing their employees. Employees are frequently placed directly in a working role and are expected to pursue the necessary information and skills on their own. This is not to say that American workers do not expect their companies to be committed to training and development. On the contrary, most Americans consider it their right. Professional development is seen as a necessary benefit, much like health insurance, which is automatically provided by many companies. The difference between American and Japanese expectations of training is rooted in the two cultures' differing views regarding the place of training in the life of the worker.

Japanese Perspective

In Japan, large companies assume that employees are loyal; therefore, the company invests in their development with the expectation of a lifetime of service. This is still the case despite the recent spurt of layoffs in Japan. Many Japanese see the company as a kind of extended family that takes care of the workers throughout their lives in exchange for dedication and loyalty. Great value is placed on the ideal of lifetime employment and permanent job security. Japanese managers coming to the United States have heard that Americans have high turnover rates, but they assume that human nature (from their perspective) will cause the Americans to develop loyalty to Japanese companies because of the presumed expectation that employment will last a lifetime. They think that the American labor market will change radically as a result of their positive (from their perspective) influence.

When Japanese managers are confronted by the reality of high worker mobility in the United States even within Japanese-owned companies, their fundamental concept of human nature is shaken. It's often a shock to them that Americans value the nature of their work and the opportunity to advance rapidly over job security or lifetime employment. Because the Japanese are not used to dealing with that sort of workforce, their first reaction tends to be to reduce financial investment in training and development. That reaction is based on clear statistics about the loss of their investment, but it also raises questions about how to train a highly mobile workforce.

When they finally do decide to initiate training, they often treat everyone in the organization like a beginner. In the Japanese experience, most newly hired workers *are* beginners and need to be trained to understand the company philosophy. This perspective is reinforced by the attitude of many Japanese in upper-management positions who feel that training is necessary only for people in junior positions and that when workers reach a certain level in the Japanese organization they don't need any more training. At that point, the Japanese expect education rather than training.

In contrast to Americans, Japanese often assume that the training department is responsible for determining the training needs of the company, not the participants. As for career development, most Japanese expect patience and loyalty from their employees. Management is expected to be responsible for choosing the job and career development path which is in the best interest of both the employee and the company. Management must inspire each employee to choose and accept that development path. Employees who don't trust the company to be responsible for their career development create serious difficulties. The Japanese employee trusts that management is providing the training for some useful purpose, but they don't necessarily expect to be told what that purpose is. They don't feel the need to question management's actions as much as Americans do, nor do they expect to be strategically involved until they reach a more advanced age (typically in their forties).

From a Japanese perspective, master trainers demonstrate models for trainees to follow. During the training process, trainees follow the instructions of their trainers, who demonstrate the skills to be learned. After the master trainer demonstrates a process, the trainees are expected to practice the skill by repeating exactly what the master trainer did. This process is continued until the trainee demonstrates a level of competence recognized as adequate by the master trainer. Trainees do not usually ask questions of the trainer in the group because it may be taken as disrespectful, but they are free to ask all the questions they wish after the session, when time permits. In essence, the learning style of the Japanese is to listen, observe, and then repeat what was demonstrated. This is dramatically different from the learning style of the American: listen, clarify the information through questioning the trainer, observe, clarify with more questions, and then repeat what was demonstrated (while occasionally challenging the trainer as to why it is done this way). The Japanese assume that trainees need a high level of feedback from the trainer in order to measure their progress, but trainees do not give feedback to the trainer until the training is over—and then only if they are asked to do so by the training program administrator.

This issue of training and learning-style differences between Japanese and Americans can be further clarified with the following example. A group of American technical trainers were sent to Tokyo to train their Japanese counterparts. The American trainers were from an American producer of three-dimensional motion picture projectors. Their objective was to teach the Japanese how to run the sophisticated projectors. Given that the projectors were very expensive and highly complex, the Americans prepared a detailed training program. In the classroom, they described the operation of the projector and occasionally asked the Japanese projectionists to perform certain functions on it. While demonstrating its use, the Americans continually told the Japanese, "Please ask questions any time you need to, and feel free to stop us if you don't understand." Hearing this, the Japanese smiled and nodded, but they rarely asked questions. Assuming everything they said was understood, the Americans proceeded through the two-week training course. The Japanese attended every session, practiced using the projectors, and showed good progress.

Six months after the program ended, one of the American trainers came back to Tokyo to conduct a session for some new projectionists and found, to his surprise, that while he was gone, the Japanese had taken their million-dollar projector apart, labeled each piece and were practicing taking it apart and putting it back together. The oldest of the trainees had assumed the role of master trainer and was demonstrating this process to the new trainees. He would then have one of the other trainees repeat the task of completely dismantling and reassembling the projector. Trainees were allowed to operate the projector only after successfully completing this process. In other words, they were involved in a much more hands-on approach to training. The American approach of lecture, answer questions, demonstrate, participant practice, then lecture some more left them ill-prepared to be competent projectionists. In the words of the senior Japanese trainer, "We never felt comfortable interrupting the Americans during class time and they never slowed down the pace of training. We needed more time to study and fully understand the inner workings of the projector in order to become competent projectionists. We don't learn new skills by interacting so much, we just need to get involved with our hands." In order to learn how to operate the machine the Japanese trainees had to perform over and over again a basic function modeled for them—and it was not even a function necessary to the operation of the machine.

American Perspective

Americans are accustomed to training which starts out with an assessment of what their needs are. They assume that the training professionals are going to take that assessment and design a curriculum that directly relates to their needs. They think that, strategically, management offers training because of a specific goal that they have for the participants. They expect that the materials and the style of delivery will directly relate to the needs and skills they are supposed to be developing and that the evaluation of their success in the training will impact directly on their promotion and advancement in the company. The planned integration of training and development into career and organizational development is a strategy that the American worker assumes, and Americans expect to be involved in decisions which affect their career development. This expectation is largely a result of the great value Americans place on self-determination. Because Americans see their country as a place of freedom and opportunity, they believe that citizens should be allowed to pursue whatever career path they are capable and desirous of pursuing. The personal freedom which most Americans associate with the free market system requires that employers allow their workers to have a hand in developing and guiding their own careers.

Alternative employment opportunities outside the company are always available. Having the option to pursue them is inherent in the freedom Americans enjoy and is part of the American dream. Arbitrary and frequent movement from company to company is not, however, generally considered the best way to pursue a career. If U.S.-based Japanese companies establish a policy of involving their American employees in determining the training to be offered to them and in the planning for their career development—which, as good managers, they should—then they will reap benefits in loyalty and motivation that will offset the turnover. If a company loses some of its investment when a worker leaves, then it is free to recoup that investment by hiring a well-trained worker from another company.

Americans believe that training must be targeted to those specific needs which motivate the individual trainee. This requires a great deal of information to be shared about the company, its operations and resources, the market and the customer, and other relevant data. Each employee wants to understand his or her role in the company as a whole. This knowledge will serve as a motivational force for American employees in assessing and pursuing training opportunities.

In the training environment, Americans expect training to take place through interaction with the trainer. Questions, answers, opinions, and feelings are all part of the learning experience. Americans don't like to be force-fed or to feel like robots following the model of the trainer. This course of action invariably proves counterproductive. These tendencies are the result of another important American value: individuality. Americans believe that each person should be treated like an individual, not a member of a group. Furthermore, each individual is assumed to have valuable contributions to make. The importance Americans place on the assumption that every person has an equal right to express his or her point of view can be seen in the popularity of town hall meetings where high-level public officials (even the president of the United States) answer the questions of average people. If a trainer tries to deny an American worker's right to ask questions and be treated like an individual, that trainer will lose the confidence of the audience.

These kinds of learning style differences are strongly influenced by the corporate culture at headquarters and in the American subsidiary, so let's turn to an analysis of the global imperatives and the local conditions.

Step 4
Organizational Exploration

Global Imperatives   Local Conditions

Japanese	American
• The proper strategy for a younger workforce is for the company to advance them as a group • In exchange for loyalty to the company, workers receive appropriate training and career advancement • Managers should maintain tight control; top-down decisions regarding training and development	• The proper strategy for a workforce is to be highly mobile • Each worker must take responsibility for career decisions • Training should give workers more control and more options for their careers

Japanese Perspective (Global Imperatives)

The Japanese managers in this incident also had several unvoiced, fundamental assumptions which were, in their case, imposed on them from global headquarters in Japan.

1. People move up the corporate ladder from within. The newly hired employee is trained internally and promoted. Mid-career hires are rare.

2. Loyalty to the company and a sense of obligation are highly valued.

3. The overseas subsidiary should be operated as an extension of headquarters in Japan.

The first of these assumptions was that an organization-wide, lockstep approach to moving people up the corporate ladder is the best strategy for developing the careers of workers in a company. Headquarters assumed that, as in the development systems in the martial arts, it takes a set number of years for newly hired employees to obtain a basic understanding of the company. This assumption is based on the idea that the best strategy for building a company is to hire young workers and develop them from the ground up. This means that workers enter the company at the bottom of the hierarchy and are developed in such a way that they progress as a group in standardized steps up the corporate ladder. Rules regarding what to do about midcareer hires are not formulated in a Japanese company; hence, when a Japanese manager abroad enters a situation where most of his employees have been hired in the middle of their careers, there is little guidance available from headquarters. Managers who find themselves in that situation end up trying to manage their subsidiaries as though their workers were novices, which results in a significant mismatch of motivations, assumptions, and expectations.

The second imperative passed down from headquarters was the assumption of loyalty to the company on the part of the workforce—an assumption developed in the context of the reciprocal relationship known as *amae* which exists between management and workers in a Japanese organization. The existence of a reciprocal sense of *on* (obligation) and *giri* (duty) from manager to employee is a core Japanese assumption about the nature of good human relationships within any organization. In this system of thought, as a manager demonstrates commitment to employees, the employees will demonstrate loyalty to the manager.

The third assumption passed down from headquarters in this case was that the proper way to manage the company was to treat it like a Japanese organization. Japanese companies have a greater tendency to see the proper strategy of global management as tight central control. This notion of centralization implies that top management should decide what sort of training and development everyone in the organization needs. Some Japanese companies claim that the strategy for operating in the United States is Americanization—putting Americans in charge of their U.S. subsidiaries. In many cases, however, this management assumption is merely *tatemae*—the public voice of the company. The real corporate expectation, or the private voice (*honne*), is for Japanese managers in the United States to maintain tight control and allegiance to headquarters' standards and decision-making processes.

Taking all three global imperatives into consideration, the appropriate strategy for human resources development on the part of the Japanese managers in our experience is to give high value to long-term employees, to direct people into leadership roles who demonstrate loyalty, and to inculcate in them headquarters' vision, strategies, and culture.

American Perspective (Local Conditions)

In protesting the approach which their managers took toward training and development in the Silicon Valley Japanese company, the American workers were strongly influenced by assumptions about strategy which were imposed on them by local conditions. The strong individual ethic of the American workplace requires each worker to take personal responsibility for his or her career path and skill development. This feeling of self-reliance is much more prevalent than a sense of being cared for by one's supervisor or manager. This is not a matter of trust but rather of reality. Having a genuine mentor to take care of one's career and development is beyond most Americans' expectations and, indeed, contrary to their common sense assumptions. In fact, employees who do not take personal initiative for developing their careers are often assumed by employers and managers to be lacking in ambition and motivation.

In addition, midcareer changes of employment are often the rule rather than the exception. If such choices are not productive from the employee's perspective—if they do not capitalize on the employee's strength and if performance is not adequately rewarded—the employee is likely to seek work elsewhere.

Step 5
Conflict Resolution

Concerned that the continuing conflict over training and development would have a negative impact on the level of morale and rate of turnover, the American human resources manager decided to intervene. The first step was to initiate an assessment of the problem through personnel interviews. In this she was assisted by an able Japanese employee assigned to support the human resources office. The data they collected moved them through the first four of the seven problem-solving steps as outlined in chapter 2: problem identification, problem clarification, cultural exploration, and organizational exploration. They were then able to turn to the conflict resolution process.

After the data was examined, it became clear that the heart of the conflict lay in the discordance between local conditions in the United States and the global imperatives of the Japanese parent company. In order to bridge this gap, the human resources team set up a series of meetings patterned on the cross-cultural conflict resolution model (see chapter 2), with the two of them serving as mediators. The first round consisted of monocultural groups in which the Japanese and Americans, among themselves, were able to vent their feelings about the other group, making accusations and passing judgments, without doing harm.

During this round of meetings, participants were given two assignments to do in their monocultural groups. First, they were to explain what the local (American) employees expected relative to training and development and to describe the logic which drove American behavior. The second was to do the same for the Japanese perspective. The only ground rule was that the explanation for each culture had to identify the *positive* intention behind the behavior or attitudes. They were assisted in this by the bicultural team serving as facilitators or mediators, who emphasized the importance of understanding that each side in a cross-cultural conflict has a logic which drives its behavior but that this logic is usually not carefully explained and is not understood by the other culture. To underline this point, the American human resources manager explained to the Japanese participants the logic which determines the attitudes of Americans toward training and development. Just as important, she was then able to describe to the Japanese participants in an objective nonconfrontational manner how Americans reacted to some of the Japanese attitudes toward training and development.

The Japanese cofacilitator did the same for the Americans in their monocultural group. The result was that the members of each group began to question their assumptions about not only how best to deal with training and development but how to interpret and manage conflict as well.

The next step was to bring the two sides together in bicultural groups. Here the Japanese and American mediators facilitated an unemotional discussion of their differing perspectives. Out of this emerged a new understanding of perceptual and value differences and of differences in organizational expectations, all of which served to generate mutual respect and an increasing sense of harmony.

In this new atmosphere, the two groups committed themselves to creating a strategic plan for training and development which integrated corporate imperatives and local conditions. This meant that they would have to establish a training system which met the requirements of corporate headquarters, while meeting expectations of the Americans.

To accomplish this aim, a strategic planning workshop was scheduled. One of the first things the group discovered was that two of the things the Americans wanted ran parallel to the interests of the Japanese: (1) they wanted to know what management thought about their career paths and (2) they expressed a desire to understand the company in its global context—the products, assumptions, values, visions, and future plans of the company as they were perceived in Japan.

For their part, the Japanese realized that, by taking responsibility for themselves, the Americans were merely doing what was necessary for them to survive in the local workplace. They wanted to support the American sense of responsibility for self so that the company would have strongly motivated, creative, initiative-taking workers who could do their jobs in competitive ways. It became important for the Japanese managers to hear from their American workers what their expectations were for their own careers and what their own skill needs were. This would allow the Japanese managers to make better decisions about appropriate training and development strategies.

The Japanese management further discovered that there were many reputable training firms in the United States which could provide excellent training for their personnel. They also began to recognize the importance of allowing Americans to pursue higher education goals at accredited institutions. The Americans for their part came to a greater appreciation of the kind of corporate training they could get from headquarters and from their local Japanese managers.

One issue which remained unresolved was the question of the training style exhibited by the Japanese trainers, which was incompatible with American expectations and needs. In order to solve this problem, the cultural mediators agreed to work with the Japanese trainers to help modify their approach to training so that it better suited the Americans.

Step 6
Impact Assessment

As the new training and development strategy was carried out, the human resources manager assessed its effectiveness in resolving the conflict and found the Americans doing well. After appropriate training, they scored high on tests gauging their acquisition of knowledge about the corporation, about its product, vision, strategy, customer relations, and style. During the strategic planning workshop, she built a list of key learnings the Japanese wanted the Americans to have, and the Americans greatly exceeded Japanese expectations in mastering them. Wishing to learn from management what management wanted to teach them was a new motivation for the American workforce, though it was a kind of quid pro quo for the Japanese willingness to learn how to adapt to local American conditions. As the new strategy mandated, the results of each of the training sessions were carefully assessed. Surprisingly, the Americans achieved high scores (from their perspective) in learning the Japanese language, reflecting the importance they had come to place on improving their ability to communicate with the representatives from headquarters.

Although employee attitude surveys demonstrated that the new strategy was having a positive impact on the morale of the American workers, there were indications that the Japanese managers were not entirely satisfied that the training programs were benefiting the company. To solve this problem the HR manager modified the training program assessment instrument so that it revealed how the trainees' new skills had contributed to improving company operations—which satisfied the Japanese managers.

The new strategy resulted in a number of benefits to the company. First, learning about the corporate culture produced an increase in the loyalty the Americans felt toward the company. Second, there was an improvement in employee morale, which resulted in demonstrably lower turnover rates. Finally, both the workers and the managers were satisfied that the individual training programs were bringing new and better skills into the company workforce.

One example of the consequences of the strategy involved the training of the Americans to be more effective in making presentations and proposals to Japanese headquarters. Two Americans had been to Tokyo twice to try to convince headquarters executives to spend five million dollars on a new marketing campaign in the Unites States but had failed both times. Their U.S. superiors believed the failure was caused in part by an excess of enthusiasm (by Japanese standards). They simply oversold their idea. The Americans were told during training that in the Japanese corporate world, too much enthusiasm is a sign of immaturity. The Americans were shown how to restrain themselves and were advised to structure a more formal presentation with additional graphics, statistics, and details—and less hyperbole. Their third trip to Japan was successful—and the campaign generated a huge upswing in the sales of the American subsidiary!

Step 7
Organizational Integration

During the conflict resolution process, the mediators had generated a number of reports which were disseminated by the human resources department to the others in the organization. The achievements of the training programs, from both headquarters and outside vendors, were also written up in the company's newsletter. This documentation created a lasting curriculum which could be used by the managers to help make future training decisions. Individual results of training programs were also recorded and, when added to personnel files, contributed to the performance appraisal process.

The company celebrated the resolution of the conflict during its annual sales meeting, and the positive outcomes of individual training programs were also published in the company newsletter. Personal success stories were told, and managers reminded their workers of the benefits of their new training and development strategy, the most significant of which was the five-million-dollar commitment from headquarters.

While the original conflict had occurred in the sales and marketing division of the company, top management had been involved from the outset, and when they saw the positive results of the new strategy, they moved quickly to implement similar training and development strategies throughout the entire corporation. This is a step in the maximization of benefits from conflict resolution which more Japanese managers in U.S. subsidiaries need to make.

5

Corporate Structure

Case Study: Responsibility and Authority

Defining and clarifying the *corporate structure* and the relationship between authority and responsibility are the biggest challenges facing the U.S.-based Japanese company. Assumptions about role functions are usually unwritten and unexpressed until there is a conflict. The unwritten rules which govern the assignment of authority and responsibility to managers in Japanese and American companies often go unexplained and create problems involving unclear expectations. Specifically, the assumptions held by Japanese and Americans about how much authority, if any, should be delegated along with increased responsibility vary substantially, often resulting in extreme levels of frustration when Japanese and Americans work together. This frustration eventually has a negative impact on the morale and productivity of employees, leading to high employee turnover (among Americans), especially at executive and other levels that require direct interaction between Americans and Japanese.

Structural assumptions may also be misleading when we differentiate between an individual manager's authority and the authority of a group of managers at a similar level. American organizational structure implies certain levels of independent authority for each individual manager according to his or her role in the organizational chart, whereas Japanese refer more to the authority held collectively by a certain group of managers at a particular level in the organization. Hence, American managers in Japanese companies who are given relatively important titles on the organizational chart will very likely be wrong to assume any level of independent authority apart from that shared by the group of managers at their level in the company. The interdependence among horizontally similar roles in the structure of the Japanese organization may also be experienced in vertical relationships, where consensus (Japanese style) is considered essential.

Step 1
Problem Identification

A. Statement of the Problem

There are at least two sources of frustration for Japanese managers and their American employees in U.S.-based Japanese companies when dealing with assumptions about responsibility and authority. First, Americans expect and give more explicit instructions when delegating tasks and assigning roles, while the Japanese tend to give fewer specific directions and have vaguer role expectations. Second, Americans and Japanese don't share the same assumptions about what amount of authority a manager has in a particular level in the structure of an organization. In Japanese companies, aside from top executives, it is customary for no one person to enjoy too much authority. Authority is usually spread among a number of people in a group, which means that authority resides in the collective, not the individual. The clout Japanese managers and workers carry with them to accomplish a task is usually more dependent upon the power of the group they represent or the relationships they have developed over the years with their coworkers than upon any factor of independent authority created by title, rank, or level.

Americans normally like to have a clear understanding of the authority that goes along with any responsibilities given them. It is not uncommon in American companies, however, to delegate responsibility from manager to subordinate without the authority to act independently. At the time a task is assigned, one or more of the following usually occurs: (1) the manager will clearly explain how much authority the subordinate has and what steps to take in case someone questions that authority; (2) the subordinate will clarify with the manager how much authority has been delegated; and (3) when the manager and employee know each other well or have worked together a long time, the degree of authority one has may be common knowledge so that neither of them needs to clarify the issue any further.

B. Description of the Incident

A Japanese company which had recently set up a subsidiary in the United States recruited an American executive from a large U.S. corporation. The American was hired as the vice president of American operations, reporting to a U.S.-based Japanese who was president of the subsidiary. The American was given a corner office, executive benefits, and a considerable salary increase, which the Japanese felt to be quite generous. In addition to running the business operations, the Japanese asked the American to serve as the point of contact for the local community and the media. The Japanese president intended for the American to move up to the position of senior vice president when the president returned to Japan. One year later, the Japanese, as planned, gave the American the title of senior vice president and left for Japan to become a senior executive at headquarters, in charge of all U.S. operations. Soon afterward, headquarters relocated a Japanese manager to work directly under the American as vice president of the subsidiary. Although the American was of higher rank than the new Japanese vice president, the Japanese gradually began to exercise more power and influence than the American. The American, for instance, was instructed by headquarters to get his Japanese vice president's signature on purchase orders which exceeded a certain amount. Eventually, headquarters asked the American to concentrate more on community and media relations than on managing operations, for which the Japanese manager assumed increasing responsibility. A year later, the American suddenly declared that, if headquarters intended to continue reducing his authority, he would have to resign.

The former Japanese president at headquarters was very upset to hear this but was also upset by the way his American successor had handled the situation.

> He was too pushy and demanding. How could he expect to earn the respect and trust of the management in Japan in such a short time? After all, he had only been in the company two years and only one year as a senior vice president, plus, he never kept me informed of his progress. The Japanese manager who worked under him had fifteen years of experience with the company, so naturally he was trusted more. Also, the American was always complaining that he had no authority. None of us ever enjoys a great deal of authority. We have to rely on the relationships we have developed over many years in order to get things accomplished. It is very naive and shortsighted of him to expect to have complete control over the business.

The American senior vice president was equally unhappy. "When I was hired to run the business operations," he said,

I was told that I would take over after my Japanese boss went back to Japan. Little did I know that a replacement from Japan, my supposed subordinate, would actually take the bulk of the operations away from me. I now feel like nothing more than a figurehead, to be paraded in front of the community to show the virtues of the supposedly successful blend of Japanese and American cultures we have achieved. And, to add insult to injury, I have to get my subordinate's signature on purchase orders of a certain size. Even worse, when my direct subordinate is out of the office, I have to get *his* subordinate—who is Japanese—to sign them. The message I thought I was receiving from Japan was that I had all of the responsibility to make this business run successfully, and I was accountable for that success or failure. Yet, I have no real authority to get anything done. Plus, management in Japan gets upset when I don't call them on a daily basis. I contact them when I need something. I think the writing is on the wall: I was not successful and my job is at stake. I have located a new job, and I feel I have no alternative but to take it. Furthermore, I think they want me to leave.

Step 2
Problem Clarification

Intentions versus Perceptions

Intentions	
Japanese	**American**
• Give the senior vice president time and assistance to become familiar with his new role • Have a senior vice president who brings a good balance of styles to the company but who blends in	• Establish effective working conditions • Exert control over the direction of the company

Perceptions	
Japanese	**American**
• The senior vice president is impatient, insensitive, and prone to complaint • The senior vice president tried to exert too much control over the company • The senior vice president was too critical of Japanese structures. He was a "lone wolf"	• Management is engaging in senseless office politics • Only people who have an "in" with Japanese management can succeed • Management no longer values my work—I am a "token"

Japanese Perspective

By placing restrictions on the American senior vice president's authority, the Japanese former president intended to give him the time and assistance he needed to become familiar with his new role. "The American was promoted to senior vice president because we felt that it was time to have an American in a top position in the company," he explained. "We didn't expect him to know every aspect of our business, so we sent a Japanese subordinate over to help him. When we did that, he complained we were taking his authority away." From the Japanese perspective, the American was impatient, insensitive, and prone to complain.

> We thought he would bring a good balance of managerial styles to the company, but we also wanted a person who would blend in rather than trying to mold this company after one where he had worked before. He should have been more patient and tried to learn more about how and why we do business the way we do. He needed to stay in closer contact with us so we could guide him. After all, he was still considered a new hire. Instead, he tried to push his own way while criticizing the Japanese way. He spends more time worrying about little things, like signing limits and amounts of authority, than he spends doing his job.

American Perspective

In reacting to the restrictions placed on the authority of his new position, the American senior vice president intended to establish working conditions which would allow him to be effective. "My understanding of the duties, responsibilities, and authority of a senior vice president was obviously different from the Japanese, both here and at the home office in Japan," he complained. "At the American company where I used to work, I had a signing limit hundreds of times larger, and I never had to get my own *subordinate's* signature before the request was authorized. I was hired to do a job, and I should have been allowed to do it." From his perspective, upper management was engaged in senseless office politics designed to reduce his effectiveness. "I was handcuffed from the start because I didn't have an 'in' with the top Japanese management. I have been turned into a highly compensated token instead of a functioning manager."

Step 3
Cultural Exploration

Expectations and Assumptions

Japanese	American
• Top managers should be generalists whose authority and responsibility vary greatly according to specific situations • Individual workers operate in the interdependent context of shared responsibility and authority • Workers should defer to those who come from the high-status headquarters of an organization	• Top managers should be specialists who are granted a great deal of independent authority • Individual workers are responsible for themselves and work independently of others • Workers should treat each other respectfully, regardless of their organizational status

Japanese Perspective

As a Japanese worker climbs higher into the ranks of management, more value is placed on being a generalist, and that, from a Japanese perspective, means managing people with differing specializations. Japanese generalists are not expected to be experts in every field. American executives often feel that their superior technical knowledge gives them power in their organization, but Japanese executives place greater emphasis on the fact that they have, over time, been trusted to manage others of varying degrees of responsibility and skill. Among Japanese generalists, the lines of responsibility and authority are much more vague than they are when specialization is the norm; job descriptions of high-ranking managers in a Japanese firm are not even written down. Instead, Japanese-to-Japanese delegation carries implicit information regarding the limits of one's responsibilities in carrying out a task. The diffusion of authority and responsibility also results from the value Japanese companies place on the importance of teamwork and cooperation. In this sort of system, a single, high-ranking person is unlikely to be assigned sole responsibility for one area or one task.

Interdependence is another important value in Japanese culture. When an assignment is made, it is expected that the individual worker will operate in the context of shared responsibility and authority that is inherent in the team of which he or she is a part. Individuals are not authorized to make decisions in isolation, but they are also not required to work without support, which means that teamwork is a benefit as well as a responsibility. Members of a team must work together and achieve consensus, but they also feel comfortable relying on each other to be caretakers in times of need. If one member of the team needs to be away from work because of illness or personal problems, the other members of the team work harder to make up for that person's absence. A similar situation arises when one's work is criticized by one's boss. Since all the members of a Japanese team share responsibility for all areas, they do not feel the need to defend personally a particular position or area when they are criticized by their superiors. Instead, the members of a team often accept the criticism of the supervisor as a message to the whole group and work harder to improve the situation. Ultimately the highest-ranking individual holds responsibility (*sekinin*) for the whole.

The Japanese have a genuine sense of respect for the individual, but Japanese society is founded equally strongly on the Confucian concept of honoring authority and social status. Status and social roles in Japan are more directly reflected in communication style, behavioral standards, and lines of responsibility than they are in the United States. For example, in a Japanese company in Japan, subordinates are not supposed to argue or debate with the manager when receiving criticism or when a decision is being conveyed. By arguing with a decision made by the manager, the subordinate is disregarding the hierarchical difference between their two positions. In other words, the subordinate isn't showing the proper respect due to a superior and is actually seen as insubordinate or untrustworthy. In the case of the American senior vice president, this value came into play when headquarters sent a Japanese manager to work under the American. Because his rank in the subsidiary was higher than the rank of the Japanese manager, the American assumed he had more authority. What he did not realize was that his Japanese "subordinate" actually enjoyed more status because he had been a member of the management team at headquarters in Japan. In other words, in spite of the fact that the Japanese had a less prestigious job title in the United States, headquarters gave him authority because he came from a higher-status part of the organization than the American and had been with the company for many more years.

American Perspective

There were three primary values influencing the behavior of the American senior vice president in this case: (1) job specialization, (2) self-reliance, and (3) sense of equality.

Americans tend to spell out clearly the boundaries of their job and work within those boundaries. When a task calls for skills outside one's area of specialization, it is not uncommon to rely on another person for whom those skills are a specialty. This is not to say that Americans don't work in teams and never work outside their area of specialization, but the decision to do so is usually based upon discussions among the team members. In the case of the American senior vice president, it is important to note his assumption that specialized responsibility carries with it independent authority. He assumed that when an individual is assigned a particular job, that person will be given all the authority necessary to accomplish the task.

In the American mind, people are and should be responsible for themselves. They should not depend on others to meet their needs. The world is full of risks that they must deal with as independent, self-reliant individuals. This is the American definition of maturity, and it is what children are encouraged to strive for. Americans find the work situation fraught with risk. Wrong actions or wrong decisions can leave one isolated, unsupported, and potentially subject to termination. A mistake or two, of course, does not normally result in the termination of employment, unless one fails to learn from it. There is, however, an atmosphere of insecurity in the American workplace. Thus, Americans do not easily apologize, even when they know they were wrong. To Americans, the sentence "I am sorry" is equivalent to "It was my fault," and this leaves them exposed to charges of incompetence. To the Japanese, on the other hand, apologies have a very different meaning. To say *domo sumimasen* (I'm sorry) does not mean, between Japanese, that one has admitted personal fault. Rather, the apology means that one is sorry that the uncomfortable set of circumstances arose.

Americans believe they have the same right as anyone else—including their company superiors—to be heard. They assume that, since they are among equals, it is acceptable behavior to discuss, debate, or even argue the merits or demerits of plans, activities, ideas, or theories. It is also acceptable to explain, excuse, or be defensive about their errors. Of course, Americans realize that companies have hierarchies with higher- and lower-level positions and that authority is distributed accordingly. As a result, they tend to temper or soften their remarks in front of the boss. Nonetheless, among Americans, subordinates and managers accept a certain amount of debating or explaining as a normal part of the communication or feedback process. When reproached or verbally attacked by a manager, the American subordinate can become obstinate, since the value of equality has been compromised.

Step 4
Organizational Exploration

Global Imperatives	Local Conditions

Japanese	American
• New hires should take at least a year to learn about the company and build a network of relationships before they act • Even top managers should stay in constant contact with their "foreign" subordinates	• Top managers must act quickly and decisively in order to be seen as credible American leaders • Top managers are independent actors whose authority should not be undermined by their "foreign" subordinates

Japanese Perspective (Global Imperatives)

The Japanese president in this case was influenced by a number of global imperatives, spoken or unspoken. Perhaps the most significant of these was the headquarters organization's assumption that any new person who comes into the company should take at least a year to learn about the company before exerting influence. And even after learning about the company, the new executive must learn the art of exerting influence, which takes years to develop. The Japanese president expected his American protégé to take the time to observe and experience every aspect of the company's operations during the yearly production cycle before he started making significant decisions. This meant that the American manager was expected to observe the actions of both his superiors in Japan and his subordinates in the United States. As the new person in the organization, it was his job to learn from those who were more experienced. The American's lack of experience with the company was made even more acute by the fact that he had no previous experience as a senior vice president. From headquarters' perspective, someone who was recently promoted had as much of an obligation to watch, look, and listen before making decisions as someone who was new to the company. This imperative had as much to do with fitting into the informal structure of a Japanese organization as with learning the corporate culture—the American was expected to take his time building up the network of people with whom he would confer and reach consensus on his important business decisions. Unfortunately, to the Japanese, it seemed that the American's behavior became more abrasive as time passed.

Another structural imperative passed on to the Japanese president by the headquarters organization was the expectation that the American would stay in constant communication with his boss in Japan. The American had been told to keep in touch, but he felt that weekly communication was adequate. As time went by, contact became even less frequent. From headquarters' perspective, this was unacceptable. Becoming the top person in the subsidiary did not change the fact that headquarters expected the American to confer with his superiors and make decisions by consensus.

American Perspective (Local Conditions)

The American senior vice president was also operating under the influence of two imperatives forced upon him by local conditions: (1) to be independent and (2) to produce results by implementing changes.

First, there was great pressure on him to be a visible and independent American leader. For the Americans in the Japanese subsidiary, placing an American in a position of top management was a necessary step in proving that there was no "glass ceiling" keeping Americans from promotion. In order for the presence of the American senior vice president to have true meaning to his subordinates, however, he had to prove that he had been granted independent authority. The concept of leaders as visionary independents who stand outside the crowd and lead from on high is an important facet of American business expectations. In particular, workers in companies which are owned or influenced by non-American organizations feel compelled to prove that they are not being unduly affected by the "foreign" power. The American felt that he was literally sandwiched between the Japanese and expected to report much too frequently to his superiors in Japan and, at the same time, to tolerate a Japanese subordinate continuously looking over his shoulder.

Second, the American senior vice president was under local pressure to produce short-term results. Americans like change. In fact, it could be argued that Americans place such a value on change and new ideas that change in and of itself can be regarded as good. Knowing this, the American senior vice president knew he had to move quickly in order to solve problems and keep the respect and trust of his American employees and peers. Rapid change is positively regarded in an industry where rapid change is necessary in order to survive, and the American felt that the Japanese were reducing his ability to be successful. If a new leader took a long time getting to know the company and did not immediately implement changes that were called for, many American companies would start looking for a replacement. Such a person would also fail to capture the trust and respect of subordinates, who would expect that the new leader had been brought in because he represented new ideas. This represents a strong mandate for decisive leadership, which he was prepared to give.

Step 5
Conflict Resolution

When he heard that the American senior vice president was planning to resign, the former Japanese president in Tokyo immediately flew back to the States to meet with his unhappy subordinate. When he arrived, he asked the American if he would consider meeting with a consultant with whom the president had worked in the past. The former president emphasized that he accepted part of the responsibility for the American's unhappiness and suggested that they would all benefit from such a meeting. The American agreed.

After extensive interviewing and information gathering (which provided the data for the problem identification, problem clarification, cultural exploration, and organizational exploration steps preliminary to this conflict resolution process), it became clear that the best next step would be a role clarification meeting between the Japanese president, the American senior vice president, and his "subordinate," the Japanese vice president.

At this kind of meeting Japanese group dynamics suggest that one approach to achieving harmony is for each person to convey a sense of vulnerability. Ideally, this triggers in the others the innate inclination to help those who are in a vulnerable position. The three men in this instance were able to explain to each other how they had been confused, frustrated, and hampered by their inability to make the situation work to their satisfaction. Each was also able to explain how his culture and his particular situation led him to behave in the manner he had. This continued until all three had developed a degree of understanding and empathy for the position of the others. At the end of the discussion, each person was able to apologize to the others for what had occurred. A key point shared with the American had to do with the nature of Japanese apologies. Apologies, as noted above, do not necessarily mean a person is accepting responsibility for having caused something to happen. Rather, it may mean simply an acceptance of mutual culpability and a sense of sorrow that a misunderstanding occurred at all.

Since the fact had already been established that the American would like to continue working with the company if he could resolve the question of authority and that the Japanese desired to retain the services of the American, it was not difficult, given the harmony that had been achieved, for them to accept a common goal: that they seek to establish an atmosphere of commitment, trust, and open communication sufficient for them to implement a new, expeditious, consensus-based decision-making process.

In further meetings, the group eventually arrived at an agreement consisting of five specific points.

1. The Japanese president agreed that he would bring the American to Tokyo for two months for an orientation to the corporate culture and an opportunity to build a network of relationships at headquarters.

2. The consultant agreed to provide an in-depth orientation to the American marketplace for the Japanese vice president.

3. The three men agreed that they would make future decisions by consensus. In particular, the American received assurances that decisions would not be made without his involvement. The American and the Japanese vice president decided to have weekly meetings to discuss current and future decisions for the subsidiary. As part of this agreement, they decided to contact the Japanese former president before and after their meetings so that they would both understand headquarters' perspective and to place a conference call to him in Japan if they could not resolve their problems themselves. The Japanese former president agreed to give the American the title of president of the subsidiary, which brought more prestige and greater compensation in exchange for accepting limits on his authority.

4. They agreed to implement a new system which would ensure that new Japanese arrivals at the subsidiary would engage in role clarification exercises with their American coworkers.

5. They agreed to send several key American managers to Japan for one month for an orientation to the corporate culture.

Step 6
Impact Assessment

The American did spend two months at headquarters in Japan and came back with a more thorough understanding of the culture of the headquarters organization. He also developed a network of contacts with whom he could deal directly on issues related to the operations of the subsidiary. As a result of this and the orientation sessions offered to the Japanese vice president, both felt better about their ability to interact successfully with members of the other culture. The human resources manager designed and implemented training and orientation programs for other key managers in the subsidiary. As time passed, the Japanese former president became satisfied that his two subordinates were working together as a team.

The human resources manager also elaborated on the plan by requiring each department head to provide a schedule for the training and orientation of every new person coming into the organization. In this fashion, he was able to keep track of the training and orientation process and ensure that all the members of the organization received the proper attention.

As time passed, positive results began to flow from the new organizational structure. First, the consensus-based decision-making process allowed both the American president and the Japanese vice president to come to agreement on important decisions. Customer surveys indicated that the subsidiary's clients were happy to see this managerial unity with the result that they began to feel comfortable asking questions of *either* the Japanese or the American members of management. In addition, the new policy resulted in more socializing between the Japanese and the Americans. They talked more and communicated more openly; more information being shared resulted in better business decisions. Finally, an important cultural dimension: by not losing the services of his American protégé, the Japanese president at headquarters saved face.

Step 7
Organizational Integration

In order to ensure that these efforts were organizationally integrated, a continuous flow of information about the experiences of all the managers involved in the policy formation and orientation programs was provided in the company newsletter.

Further, the consensus-based decision-making process developed out of the conflict resolution was embodied in the manager's handbook used by every manager in the company.

At the end of his two months in Japan, the company held a banquet in the American president's honor, celebrating the new relationships. The Japanese vice president had a similar celebration at the end of his two-month orientation. It was further decided that the American president would from then on visit headquarters in Tokyo twice a year to sustain his relationships there.

The impact of these steps was dramatically expanded by a number of subsequent events. The management team in the States was sent to Japan one by one for a month's orientation at headquarters. At the U.S. subsidiary, orientation using role clarification exercises was required of all incoming Japanese and their American coworkers. The model of consensus-based decision making was systematically applied at all executive management meetings. The employee's handbook was revised to contain a summary statement about the new management structure and advice to all company personnel on application of certain principles of intercultural communication. Finally, the subsidiary offered a basic training course in intercultural communication which all employees were required to take during their first six months in the company.

Staffing Policies

Case Study: Promotion Pace and Compensation Growth

*O*rganization staffing involves making strategic decisions about the characteristics of the organization. This means choosing not only which people but also which skills and qualities should be placed in particular positions. The decision to hire a new employee (especially in an upper-managerial position) can strongly influence the values and operational styles exhibited by the company; managers can use promotion and compensation to reward those employees who best exemplify the desired corporate culture. Through hiring and firing, reward and punishment, company leaders mold their organizations into what they see as effective corporate cultures. Hence, the process of staffing an organization is a process of creation and control. Not surprisingly, then, conflicting cultural assumptions can have disastrous consequences for staffing decisions in a global organization. Decisions about which roles are assigned to expatriates in a subsidiary organization, how far up the ladder a foreign national will be able to climb in the global corporation, and whether to bring in candidates from the outside for an upper-management position are decisions which result in challenging consequences for both the assignees and those with whom they work. The staff characteristics of a Japanese subsidiary in the United States push the structure of the organization into unique and dynamic circumstances which often involve conflicting cultural values and assumptions.

As we explained in the previous chapter, role expectations are often in conflict when managers from Japan and America are in a vertical relationship in the structure of a business organization. The fact that so many global companies try to operate with parallel Japanese and American structures in their subsidiaries is a testimony to the difficulties of integrating two cultures into one hierarchy. Japanese expatriates are far more easily trusted by headquarters' leadership—their performance has already been proven worthy of respect. It is rare indeed to find a start-up subsidiary headed by an American. Staffing a subsidiary with expatriate management, however, can send the message that the home office in Japan doesn't trust the local personnel. When Japanese companies in the United States set forth in the 1980s on their mission of "Americanization," their predominant objective was to solve the problems of expatriate management by selecting Americans who could ultimately take charge of their subsidiaries. This staffing strategy reflected the positive intention of providing their subsidiaries with American leadership.

Very few Japanese companies, however, were prepared for the complications and struggles that this strategy has caused. As staffing decisions created situations in which Japanese and Americans up and down the organizational line were reporting to each other, complications became overwhelming. The complications were found in a variety of areas. As we saw in the last chapter, in some cases the American had a position which was superior to the Japanese from a hierarchical perspective, but the Japanese "shadow manager" actually had more authority or clout in the organization. There were also questions about which language to use, or whether or not an interpreter was necessary. In many cases, meetings consisting of only Japanese were viewed with suspicion by the Americans. In fact, most of the specific issues examined in this book reflect in some degree problems which have resulted from these challenges.

As a defense mechanism against this kind of cultural integration and in an attempt to reduce the inevitable friction, parallel Japanese and American organizational structures (e.g., two vice presidents of finance, one Japanese and one American) were instituted. Unfortunately, the result was disastrous in many cases, especially when Japanese subordinates skipped over American superiors in order to report to other Japanese, which for the Americans indicated a lack of trust and respect. In response, Americans began to do the same.

To further compound the problem of parallel or shadow management systems, some actions on the part of the Japanese caused many Americans to feel "out of the loop" of control. For example, the tendency of the Japanese to dissuade the Americans from learning or improving skills in the Japanese language were interpreted by the Americans as a lack of trust and a sign of deviousness and secretiveness on the part of the Japanese.

Also, a double standard between corporate headquarters and subsidiaries regarding acceptable professional styles also developed. Headquarters in Japan made decisions about the U.S. subsidiaries and their customers without involving them. As a result, the American subsidiaries felt dominated—their input wasn't solicited or incorporated into strategic decisions. This further prevented the integration of business operations and raised local customer and employee doubts about the integrity of representatives from headquarters.

When the information management and performance appraisal systems seemed to Americans to be based upon different performance standards and processes for informing and evaluating Japanese and Americans, trust and respect diminished even further. Standards of compensation and benefits for Japanese expatriates were also found to be different; the Americans felt their benefits were less generous. For example, even though the U.S. subsidiary was enforcing a wage and yearly bonus freeze, frequently the Japanese would still receive their Japan-based bonus checks. Because communication skills on both sides were inadequate to communicate corporate values across parallel cultural structures, business strategies determined unilaterally by headquarters caused subsidiary employees to feel even less trusted and respected. Of course, the lack of trust and respect had a negative impact on productivity. The incident we will describe next represents the kinds of conflicts which can arise as a result of staffing decisions, in such domains as promotion pace and compensation growth.

Step 1
Problem Identification

A. Statement of the Problem

Japanese and Americans often operate with vastly different expectations about when or how often employees should be promoted. In addition, their views differ substantially in regard to the equity and timing of changes in compensation. The pace of promotion and compensation is perceived by Americans as one of the most difficult aspects of being managed by Japanese in the United States. The problem is due to at least two fundamental differences in the business cultures of Japan and the United States: (1) frequency of promotion and (2) compensation growth.

Promotion. There are different practices in the two cultures regarding the frequency of promotion. Japanese management normally expects to offer promotions every four or five years, while Americans expect to be promoted every two to three years.

Compensation. Compensation growth is tied to performance-based evaluations in the United States, whereas the Japanese traditionally make such decisions based on years of service. Currently, many Japanese companies are integrating some merit-based decision making into their promotion and compensation practices, but few are ignoring years of service. In U.S.-based Japanese subsidiaries, these fundamentally different promotion and compensation practices are at the root of much of the frustration felt by Americans and Japanese alike.

When disagreements arise because of these differences, the resulting negative judgments lead to more than simple frustration. In many cases, they result in higher turnover among the Americans than exists in comparable American corporations. Unfortunately, misunderstandings between the Japanese and American managers about promotion and compensation practices are rarely discussed. Since the expectations and assumptions that both groups bring to these issues remain unexplored, they predictably end in a decrease in morale and productivity. In some cases—such as the one we are about to describe—honest attempts on the part of each culture to accommodate or respond to the expectations of the other end up creating even more difficulties and misunderstandings.

In the case study that follows, not only are issues of promotion and compensation at stake; there is an additional factor which adds an element of paradox to the conflict and offers even deeper insights into the complexities of cross-cultural relationships.

Americans who seek employment at U.S.-based Japanese subsidiaries are not necessarily typical of their culture. From decades of research and personal contact, we have discovered that Americans who work at Japanese companies often have different needs and expectations from those of their peers who work for American companies. For one thing, they tend to be more interested in job security and compensation equity than do other Americans. The lure of higher starting salaries is especially attractive where long-term employment is anticipated.

But these higher starting salaries are made possible by the slow rate of promotion and compensation growth in Japanese companies relative to American companies. When Americans join Japanese companies, however, the pace of promotion and compensation, as we've noted, is not discussed. The Americans therefore assume that they will be promoted every two to three years. Further, the Japanese interview process tends to favor those workers who demonstrate both compliance and flexibility. This sometimes results in the hiring of workers who, like the Japanese, value maintenance of harmony over more aggressive styles of interaction, even when the interviewer is American. In particular, Americans in Japanese companies often have both the personal inclination and the perceived need to refrain from being aggressive toward their Japanese managers. This often results in a staff of Americans who are relationship builders rather than individualists pursuing their personal self-interest. Nevertheless, when they encounter Japanese policies that go against the American cultural grain, shock and anger may follow, as it did in this case.

B. Description of the Incident

In one large Japanese subsidiary with nearly a thousand American employees and eighty-five Japanese expatriate managers, an American manager had served as the head of personnel for ten years—ever since the company began its work in the United States. This American manager had studied Japanese management practices and had worked very hard in his job to demonstrate excellence and loyalty. Realizing that the Japanese do not expect promotion as quickly as Americans, he waited patiently to be moved up to vice president of administration. Each year he received an increase in compensation based upon another year of service and the increase in the cost of living. He made great efforts to adjust to the Japanese style of management and seemed to blend in with their expectation that he not be too aggressive or independent in his decision making. Similarly, he tried to develop greater satisfaction in the American workforce through regular, incremental changes in their promotion pace and compensation growth. Each time a decision needed to be made regarding promotions or compensation, the American personnel manager took his proposal to his Japanese president in order to reach a consensus.

When the American's opportunity for promotion finally came, however, he was denied the position of vice president in favor of another American who was hired from outside the company. This new person had previous experience as a vice president of administration for a rapidly growing American company and was well known in the industry as an aggressive, "American-style" manager. When the American personnel manager expressed to his Japanese president his shock at this development, he was told that the company needed a more American style of management. He was initially reassigned to another position in a faraway plant and then ultimately given a year of support to find a job with another company.

When the new American vice president of administration arrived, he brought with him his previous associate as personnel manager. He quickly concluded that his new Japanese president wanted him to develop the American workforce in a manner consistent with American staffing policies. Specifically, he thought his role was to implement a more merit-driven compensation plan, while maintaining the job security of the workforce. Taking this perceived mandate to heart, he and his personnel manager conducted a review of the promotion pace and compensation growth in the company during the previous decade. Their findings demonstrated that the American workers in their company were not receiving promotions and increases in compensation at a rate comparable to other American companies in their industry. The new vice president held a series of meetings with representatives from the American workforce and developed a proposal that would bring the subsidiary's promotion and compensation practices into a competitive position against its American rivals.

His proposal had three components. First, a new round of promotions would be made in order to place outstanding workers in positions of leadership. Second, job descriptions would be developed for each worker and a system of merit-based pay (regardless of age, race, or gender) would be adopted. Finally, the subsidiary would fund substantial across-the-board raises in order to move the company's pay scale ahead of its competitors. All in all, it was an expensive program.

When the vice president presented this proposal to the Japanese president, he was severely reprimanded. The Japanese president criticized him for being insensitive to the need to present headquarters with a reasonable budget and ordered him to make drastic alterations. When the representatives from the American workforce learned that the changes in promotion and compensation they had expected were not going to be enacted, they were deeply disappointed; many indicated that they were going to start looking for other jobs. Soon, the tension between the American vice president and the Japanese president had risen to uncomfortable levels, and they actually avoided opportunities to communicate with each other.

"I can't understand what the problem is," the American vice president complained.

> When they brought me in here, the Japanese president said he wanted a more American approach to promotion and compensation. I knew they fired the last guy who handled that area because he was too slow and gradual, so I naturally assumed that I should implement policies which were quick and substantial. I did everything any

American manager in my situation would do—the same sorts of things that have brought me so much success in my past positions—and the Japanese president hit the roof. He acted as if he had never told me to be a normal American manager. Now I have absolutely no idea what he wants.

The Japanese president was no happier with the American's actions. "His proposal was out of step with the needs of the subsidiary," he said.

I asked him to enact policies which were more American, such as replacing workers who were causing trouble or who were not performing well. Instead of helping me to rid the workforce of troublemakers, he proposed spending an unprecedented amount of money on promotions and pay raises. That was exactly the opposite of what I wanted. If I went to higher levels of management with his proposal, they would think I had lost my mind.

Step 2
Problem Clarification

Intentions versus Perceptions

Intentions	
Japanese	**American**
• Use American-style leadership to control employees and reduce the size of the labor force • Improve the quality of the workforce • Develop worker loyalty; make the company more like an American company	• Fulfill a role by being proactive and making the company more competitive • Provide good leadership and build good relationships • Make the company more like an American company

Perceptions	
Japanese	**American**
• The American vice president has poor judgment • The American vice president's proposal will destroy worker motivation • The American vice president is willing to spend unreasonable amounts of money	• The Japanese are misinterpreting my actions as aggressive • The Japanese don't really want American leadership • The Japanese are unwilling to adopt competitive promotion and compensation policies

Japanese Perspective

For his part, the Japanese company president had expected a more aggressive, American-style vice president and personnel manager who would control the employees by realigning resources to keep the good employees and get rid of the bad ones.

> I expected several things from my American vice president. I expected him to be knowledgeable about American personnel laws and policies and also to learn quickly what our Japanese headquarters required of our American staff. We needed to improve the quality of our workforce by rewarding the good performers and denying raises to the poor ones. That is why I let the other manager go; he wasn't aggressive enough in getting rid of the poor performers. I never expected the new vice president to request an increase in the budget for salaries. We cannot afford that!

In addition, the Japanese president was concerned that his vice president wanted to promote the very people the president felt were causing problems in the first place. "I think he has misjudged our workers. I have already made a judgment about the people he wants to promote, and it is clear to me that they are not the best performers in the company." The Japanese president was also disappointed with his new vice president's inability to learn and transmit to the employees the company's principles about sacrifices necessary for the good of the whole.

> I expected our vice president to work toward developing our employees' loyalty to the company, but instead we have had many cases of unexpected turnover. He should have explained our personnel policies of promotion and compensation so as to keep our employees motivated and committed to the company. His proposal will destroy motivation by creating job descriptions that limit responsibility.

The paradoxical nature of the Japanese president's clarification of his intention served only to further complicate the issue in the American vice president's mind.

American Perspective

The American vice president felt he was fulfilling his new role by being proactive and providing his superior with the best plan for making the company more competitive in the American market. "I was surprised that my Japanese manager never tried to understand the American workplace requirements concerning personnel policies," he said. "It was very difficult to put our company in a competitive position because of the Japanese standards on compensation and promotion. I expected them to listen to my suggestions, but they kept telling me I was too aggressive." From his perspective, he was doing his best to provide the Japanese management with good leadership.

> I thought I was building good relationships with my superior by helping him understand how to remain competitive in the industry. I know how important relationships are to the Japanese, but I

guess they did not appreciate my efforts. Now they have a real problem if they think anything less than my proposal will satisfy the workforce. It doesn't pay to assume that Americans and Japanese mean the same thing by "Americanization." I was assuming that he meant we should be more like an American company in how we deal with our personnel in order to attract and keep good employees.

Step 3
Cultural Exploration

Expectations and Assumptions

Japanese	American
• Workers should be patient and wait for the company to promote them at the appropriate time, usually every five to six years • Workers at the same level should be treated similarly • Workers should be compensated on the basis of loyalty, seniority, status, and ability • American workers should not be upset by sudden firings or layoffs; it's the "American way"	• Workers should be promoted on a two- to three-year basis • Workers at the same level should be treated differently based on their ability and their accomplishments • Workers should be compensated on the basis of performance, rather than status or seniority • Japanese companies provide workers with high job security • The Japanese president should choose one style of management, not vacillate between the "American way" or "Japanese way"

Japanese Perspective

To understand Japanese promotion and compensation policies, we have to go back to Japanese perceptions of the
recruitment process. New hires in Japanese companies are
considered blank pieces of paper. Japanese companies are
looking for potential, not accomplishment—for someone who
will be a social fit within the corporate culture and who will
develop needed experience and skills over a long period of
time. Because the company recruits employees with the idea
that they will stay in the company for a long period of time (if
not their whole lives), there is little emphasis on rapid upward
mobility for individual workers. The assumption is that employees give the company their loyalty in exchange for long-
term job security and the eventual opportunity to reach a
position of high rank. Japanese employees who attain a prominent position are expected to enjoy substantial privileges, but
they are also expected to have earned the right to those
privileges through many years of loyalty and effort.

The Japanese president felt it was common sense that an
employee wouldn't be ready for a promotion for four to five
years and that compensation should be used to build good
teamwork. On the other hand, he had been in the United States
so long that he eagerly anticipated the Americanization strategy. In the United States, since promotion and compensation
can vary more significantly by merit, he was expecting the new
vice president to execute a plan within budget constraints to
build loyalty from good performers while holding back or
dismissing poor performers. The president had practiced what
he perceived to be American-style management by moving out
what he judged to be a poor performer—the old personnel
manager. When his new vice president came on board, he was
shocked to receive a proposal to increase the budget for
promotions and compensation. He had thought that becoming
competitive with American companies would happen more
slowly and had trusted the new vice president to protect the

company and himself from having to present headquarters with any rapid changes. These expectations were not communicated to or shared by the new vice president.

Patience and loyalty are the most prominent Japanese values concerning promotion and compensation. New employees are hired as a group, trained as a group, and usually promoted as a group, rather than as individuals. Because individuals do not expect to be rewarded by quick promotion or sudden leaps in compensation, they place great value on the notion that patience and loyalty will pay off in the end. In fact, this is largely true. The whole Japanese economy is geared toward the objective of full employment, even though only about 22 percent have such security. As a policy, companies have simply not fired their workers in the past. Today, because of the difficult economic situation in Japan, more and more Japanese companies are being faced with bankruptcy and layoffs. This is not to say that Japanese companies are happy about laying off their workers—this is a major emotional upheaval for both the newly unemployed and for those who must continue to work while their colleagues look for new jobs. Traditionally, Japanese companies have used time during downturns in the market to train their employees, but as a result of the rupture of the Japanese bubble economy and the recession it caused, this practice has become extremely difficult to sustain.

The Japanese value of job security is based on the ultimate priority of developing trusting working relationships. Since Japanese companies believe that the basic component of workplace trust is a feeling of mutual loyalty between management and labor, it becomes necessary to provide extended employment (formerly, lifelong) to their workers. This was one of the major sources of conflict for the president. Knowledge of the American culture and system drove him to demand an aggressive policy for compensation and promotion. However, this put him in conflict with his own deeply ingrained values of nurturance and development of his employees over many years. His attempt to switch styles and adopt a localized (American) approach put him squarely on the fence between the two cultures. This phenomenon is common with relocated managers worldwide and difficult to resolve. By not adopting more of the local practices, international managers are labeled as culturally insensitive. Unfortunately, becoming more sensitive to local demands is not a guarantee of success either. If a relocated manager adopts too many local practices, the view from the top, in many cases, is that the manager is no longer protecting the interests of the company, but has "gone native." By bringing in an American manager in the expectation that poor performers would be eased out of the company, the Japanese president in this case was violating one of the most basic tenets of Japanese management philosophy. Even though he was going against the common sense philosophy of no layoffs in Japan, he was doing his best to work within the U.S. system. Believing that what he requested of his American subordinate was normal in the United States, he was surprised that his actions brought so much negative criticism from the Americans.

American Perspective

Americans like working for leading-edge companies, where top management is articulate and inspiring, gives clear directions, and makes timely decisions in the best interests of the employees. They value managers who are honest and open with their employees in sharing information. They like bosses who invite thoughtful suggestions from their subordinates, who give rewards on the basis of merit, and who base promotions on clear performance criteria. American employees like to know where they stand and often plan to move up or out within a two- to three-year time span. These are the kinds of things that affect motivation and performance and which differentiate an excellent workforce from a mediocre one. The Japanese president in the above case had a mixed understanding of what motivates Americans. He thought he was supporting American staffing practices by firing a low performer and bringing in a hard-driving, results-oriented producer, and he expected his new vice president to meet that expectation. However, he also had some budgetary limitations and other expectations about compliance with the principles and policies from headquarters, which he did not clearly communicate to his new vice president.

The American vice president was perplexed. He thought he had a clear mandate from the president to proceed in an aggressive manner in order to create an American-style compensation structure. On the one hand, the president had fired the previous personnel manager for lack of aggressiveness. On the other, the president was upset because the vice president hadn't proceeded more judiciously when considering presenting radical changes to the home office in Japan. A clear, consistent message was all the American vice president was asking for.

As the vice president explained to the president, American workers expect to be promoted on a two- to three-year basis. Living in a society where innovation and mobility are the norm, Americans have come to value change as a positive indicator of career success. If an employee spends five years or more in the same position (or at the same level), there is a common perception that the person is not performing well. Furthermore, Americans expect more differentiation between workers who perform very well and those who are only average. This means that very competent workers expect to be compensated at a significantly higher level than their less successful peers, irrespective of job titles.

The idea that people should be compensated on the basis of performance rather than status or seniority has its roots deep in the American value system. The belief that the United States is a place where anyone can achieve success—even if born poor or in another country—is a powerful part of the American national image. Thus, the suggestion that workers should be compensated on the basis of something other than performance is offensive. Americans believe that one reason for the founding of their nation was to do away with the sort of status-based privileges traditionally enjoyed by the European aristocracy. They resent decisions based on status implied by differences of culture, race, religion, gender, and so on. In fact, such policies are against the law. This, in combination with the capitalist ideal of a level playing field, where all workers have the same opportunity to earn and achieve, has led to the development of modern-day performance-based compensation and promotion practices.

Step 4
Organizational Exploration

Global Imperatives   Local Conditions

Japanese	American
• It is important to reduce risk, even if it means dropping back to outdated management practices • It is imperative to keep expenses down whenever possible • It is important to fill management positions with American managers • Balancing the demands of the home office and subsidiary can cause the Japanese expatriate to appear inconsistent with his demands	• In order to be successful, companies must offer competitive promotion and compensation plans • High starting salaries in Japanese companies do not justify a slow rate of promotion and compensation growth

Japanese Perspective (Global Imperatives)

Many Japanese who work in U.S.-based Japanese subsidiaries have characteristics which distinguish them from their compatriots. The first of these characteristics is a tendency toward regressive, rather than progressive, management practices. When Japanese managers come to the United States and work with Americans, they tend not to follow the more modern Japanese trends in management. In an unfamiliar environment, it is much easier for them to do things the old-fashioned way. Reducing risk becomes an imperative. Rather than being clear and inspirational in their leadership, they tend to drop back into old habits, rejecting the sort of merit-based practices which are gaining popularity in Japan and which require culturally difficult performance reviews.

Another imperative for Japanese managers in the United States is to keep expenses down. American managers also try to keep expenses under control, but some Japanese go at it almost obsessively, seeing their success in doing so as a way to distinguish themselves in the eyes of their superiors. An example of obsessiveness often cited by Americans in U.S.-based Japanese subsidiaries is the practice of saving money by cutting down the number of lights in an office (every other bank of ceiling-mounted fluorescent light fixtures would be turned off). Even though this practice results in negligible cost savings, the Japanese view it as a sacrifice shared by all; it sends the message of continuous vigilance toward cost cutting. The mandate to reduce expenses while increasing profits has led to an emphasis on incremental change. Small changes are less costly and maintain workplace harmony.

Finally, Japanese managers in the United States know the importance of Americanization. Finding Americans who can fill top leadership positions is the first step toward grooming an American to take over the subsidiary. Not only does American management reduce the cost of maintaining Japanese expatriates, it also satisfies a complaining workforce which would rather deal with a familiar, American top manager.

American Perspective (Local Conditions)

We have noted above the paradox that is central to the conflict being described here. This paradox ultimately became so pronounced that it constituted an important local condition which had to be understood before harmony could be achieved. The paradox lay in the degree to which Americans who work for U.S.-based Japanese subsidiaries tended—in contrast to their counterparts who work for American companies—to place great value on job security and pay equity. While their perspective did not provide for the firing of poor performers, it did include a promotion, compensation, and benefits package competitive with other companies in the industry.

The paradox, of course, lies in the fact that the Americans who worked for the company, while generally attuned to Japanese management styles and organizational policies, found that when faced with the crisis brought about by the conflict between the president and vice president, they reverted to their primary American values. The longer they worked in a Japanese company and experienced the Japanese practice of slow promotion and incremental salary increases (and falling further behind the rest of the employees in the industry in salary and position), the more they realized how much the Japanese policy was in conflict with traditional American values. Confronting the differences in another culture often makes people realize how much they appreciate the uniqueness of their own culture or at least understand the strength of cultural influence. In short, the employees recognized immediately the desirability of the aggressive new promotion and compensation system.

Step 5
Conflict Resolution

Conflicts about promotion pace and compensation growth often arise during attempts by U.S.-based Japanese subsidiaries to institute a policy of Americanization, which for many Japanese companies means putting Americans in charge of other Americans. But the placing of Americans in positions of top management is only the first step in creating a solution to the problem of good leadership in the subsidiary. The next step is to realize that Americans in such positions need a great deal of cultural education to understand the expectations of the Japanese organization. Unfortunately, few Japanese companies are effective in clarifying and explaining their expectations to their American managers. Similarly, few American managers realize that they need to strive as rapidly as possible to understand Japanese practices and determine what expectations their superiors have of them.

Frustrated that there had been such a complete breakdown of communication between himself and his Japanese president, the American vice president sought help from the authors as external consultants. The vice president explained that he was concerned not only about the level of tension in the company but about his job as well. After some delicate negotiations and in-depth interviews with the two men, the authors concluded that the first step in the resolution of the conflict must be a meeting with the president and vice president designed to create a mutual understanding of how the breakdown in communication came about. In essence, the meeting involved taking them through the first three steps in our process: problem identification, problem clarification, and cultural exploration.

Once two people have a mutual understanding of the origins of their conflict, it is possible for them to develop a sense of shared responsibility for breakdowns that occur. In this case, we encouraged each of the men to identify and clarify the cultural basis of the problem for the other. Through this process, each came to realize that he was operating with stereotypes about the other. The Japanese president realized that he had expected the American vice president to behave in certain ways. Not having explored with any American what Americanization means in the United States, he realized he had assumed that it simply meant having an American in a leadership position. For his part, the American understood that what he had learned about Japanese culture in the past had led him to expect his Japanese president to place great emphasis on maintaining job security. Instead of discussing the meaning of Americanization with his Japanese superior, the vice president had acted on his assumption that job security for employees of the local subsidiary would be more important to the president than budgetary considerations. Both men realized that they had reacted negatively to the other's actions because they had differing ideas of what constituted common sense in business. This was a good example of how a superficial knowledge of the other culture's values can lead to conflict. Both parties thought they knew what the other wanted, but neither had taken the time to clarify expectations or discuss the consequences of their respective strategies. Neither of them had clarified the issues. The American assumed he understood what his boss wanted; the Japanese assumed his message was clear to his subordinate.

Recognizing that they were both at fault for the breakdown in communication, they first apologized to each other for allowing the conflict to continue so long and then went out to dinner in order to begin the process of getting to know each other better. Realizing that they had not made a practice of seeing each other informally, they also resolved to have dinner together at least once a month. At this first dinner, they actually discussed very little business, using the time to get to know each other and share personal information. After several of these casual dinners, they scheduled a second formal meeting to continue the process of resolving their conflict over promotion and compensation. Since they had achieved some degree of rapport at the dinners, it was possible for us to take them through an exercise on setting expectations during the second meeting.

The aim of the exercise was to clarify the meaning of "Americanization" and to resolve the conflict between the two men over their differing perceptions of applying Americanization in the company. In order to resolve this conflict, it was necessary for each man to explain his concept of Americanization and his expectations regarding its initiation into the company. The Japanese president explained that, although he wanted the subsidiary to be competitive in the American marketplace, he also wanted to maintain the values and adhere to the imperatives of headquarters in Tokyo. For his part, the American vice president explained that, while he understood the need for the subsidiary to reflect the values of headquarters, he was more focused on making the company competitive in the United States. He had assumed that in the spirit of applying the values of headquarters, he was not free to terminate employees who didn't perform their jobs well. After some discussion, the two men agreed that their common goal for the subsidiary was to retain the fundamental principles of the Japanese organization, which made the company unique, while at the same time to run it in a manner that would make it competitive in the American marketplace.

Once the president and the vice president arrived at a common goal, they began to discuss the steps required to achieve their vision. They agreed that the American vice president must understand the mindset of the parent company. They also agreed that headquarters must understand what the subsidiary should do to be competitive in the American marketplace. The Japanese president suggested that the American accompany him on his next trip to Japan. By doing this, the vice president could acquire a better understanding of the company's principles, operational procedures, and corporate culture. At the same time, he could help the president educate headquarters about personnel practices in the United States, particularly the link between merit pay and job descriptions. Working together, the two men could explain to headquarters what a Japanese subsidiary in the United States has to do in order to be competitive. The role of the vice president in such a process would be as a provider of facts, not as a persuader. The American would lay out the figures and talk about the consequences of not being competitive, while the Japanese president would work toward obtaining permission for an increase in the personnel budget.

Prior to the trip to Japan, a third meeting was necessary to ensure that the president understood and agreed with the vice president's plan for making the subsidiary more competitive. The first step in this process was to set expectations for how the American vice president would operate in the future, with special emphasis on the importance of keeping lines of communication open between them. For his part, the American vice president provided the president with an overview of common staffing policies in their industry. Then they agreed on the steps necessary to put together a sound proposal to headquarters that they could present clearly and defend.

They authorized a benchmark study of how their American and U.S.-based Japanese competitors dealt with promotion, compensation, job descriptions, and merit-based reward systems. They then compared their findings to the personnel practices used in Japan by the largest corporations. The idea was for the president to hear for himself from other personnel managers in American companies what the marketplace required in terms of staffing policies. Using the information acquired, they were able to put together a general, preliminary proposal to take with them to Tokyo.

In Tokyo the American was able to get a firsthand sense of the corporate culture, its general atmosphere, and the special perspectives of the Japanese who ran it. The president and vice president received a sympathetic hearing on their proposal, were able to clarify the issues relative to staffing requirements in the American workplace, and won a modest increase in their payroll budget. They also got to know each other better, aided by the trip to Japan and a brief sojourn at a traditional Japanese inn.

Upon returning to the United States, the president and the vice president met to discuss the best way to change their staffing policies. They agreed to implement a job description procedure and a merit-based reward system, but the president was still hesitant to promote the "troublesome" individuals that the American vice president wanted in management positions. It was suggested that he meet the people involved socially and observe them on the job to see if he might form a new opinion of them. It worked, and they were soon able to implement a round of promotions. Finally, in regard to the proposed salary upgrades, the president asked his subordinate to put together a plan which spread the salary upgrades over a five-year period (the original proposal was for immediate implementation). After getting headquarters' agreement, the plan was executed.

Step 6
Impact Assessment

The resolution of the staffing conflict brought a number of benefits to the subsidiary. First, the president and the vice president developed a more positive working relationship, which was apparent to the entire staff. The tension between the two men fell away and top-level decisions became easier to make without conflict. Second, the vice president achieved a firm grounding in the Japanese corporate culture, though sometimes he had to struggle to interpret the values of that culture in the American context. For instance, the age issue was a particularly thorny problem. Even though he grew to understand why the Japanese valued age so much when considering promotions, he had to confront legal issues in the United States that forbid certain kinds of decisions based on age. Especially difficult were the confrontations he frequently had with Japanese managers who insisted on considering age when evaluating someone for promotion.

In the past, his opinion was that "it doesn't matter what the person's age is. If he or she is technically qualified, that's all that we should consider." But the Japanese wouldn't accept that justification if they knew the employee being considered for promotion was younger than they thought appropriate. A breakthrough occurred when the American was advised to change his approach. Instead of emphasizing technical skills, he decided to stress the candidate's abilities as a team player, an important Japanese value when considering promotions. Since being a team player is a sign of maturity to the Japanese, the emphasis placed on it by the American would communicate to the Japanese that that person was mature, which would offset or neutralize his or her age.

Through a series of efforts of this kind, the vice president, over time, translated the values of the culture at headquarters into American behaviors and was able to demonstrate to the president and to headquarters that both his plans and personnel were in increasingly greater harmony with the corporate culture. At the same time he won the admiration and respect of his American employees as a strong leader they could look up to.

Step 7
Organizational Integration

It is important to note here that the whole process described in this chapter occurred over a period of thirteen months. We do not want to mislead the reader into believing that all of these difficulties were miraculously cleared up after only a couple of trips to Japan, some nights on the town together, and a facilitated meeting or two.

To reinforce their accomplishments within the organization, the vice president and the president first met with the department heads to explain the new staffing policy. Next, they had a similar meeting with the members of each department on promotions and salary increases. The new policy was recorded in the company personnel handbook, and a report on the trip to Tokyo was, of course, included in the company newsletter, along with an article by the vice president outlining the key learnings he had gained from his meetings with headquarters staff. Finally, a report was compiled that outlined each stage of their conflict resolution process so that similar conflicts in the future could be resolved without outside intervention.

In his article the vice president included a description of a banquet held in his honor on his last day in Tokyo, including a picture of him singing karaoke with one of the managers from headquarters. The resolution of their conflict was celebrated at a banquet for the department heads, enabling them to participate in an important ritual acknowledging the new spirit of teamwork between the president and vice president.

Finally, the vice president, reflecting on what he had learned about the importance of cultural differences in organizational dynamics, asked the human resources department to develop a series of intercultural effectiveness workshops for their Japanese and American employees. He also had the orientation program for newly hired employees redesigned to include instruction on how to be effective in the company's bicultural environment. This effort was capped when he invited the Japanese president to give a presentation—which was videotaped and subsequently shown to all new employees—outlining the company's principles and values.

7

Performance Standards

Case Study: Performance Management and Equal Employment Opportunity

In multicultural management, *performance standards* are the most hidden of all organizational characteristics. A standard is a behaviorally measurable performance at which one rating (or judgment) changes into another rating or level. For example, with what performance level does a worker's rating change from a "3" to a "4" on a five-point scale? At what point does production go from being superior to being outstanding? Our answers to questions like these reflect the standards we use to judge performance. In order for performance-rating scales to be meaningful, each of the numbers on the scale must be linked to objective criteria that clearly show that performance quality or value has changed. Performance standards are quantifiable—they have visible indicators. When judgments are made about an individual's or a team's performance, those performers who have not been informed about the standards on which the judgment was based often cannot understand why a particular judgment was made. All too often, one person is promoted over another for what are perceived by those who do not know the standards as subjective reasons. All too often, headquarters makes decisions based on what the subsidiary perceives as subjective reasons. In each of these cases, the observers in the subsidiary react negatively because they do not understand the standards which are being used to make judgments.

Bringing performance standards into the awareness of the whole company will clarify and make accessible to objective assessment the reasons for which evaluations, judgments, and decisions are made. In cross-cultural situations, it is quite common for members of one cultural group to criticize members of another. This usually occurs when the reasoning behind unfamiliar behaviors, or the behaviors themselves, are not understood or valued. In multinational corporations, the local (indigenous) managers in the foreign subsidiary will often attribute negative intent, ignorance, or even stupidity to the reasoning of decision makers at headquarters or of visiting expatriate managers. This is in spite of the fact that, from the perspective of headquarters or expatriate managers, there may be clear, objective criteria by which certain decisions are made. Often, performance standards in one culture are thought by decision makers to be "common sense," but we know that common sense varies by culture. From a Japanese perspective it is natural, for example, to assume that workers will be motivated if management sets high goals which may or may not be immediately achievable. Americans, on the other hand, believe that what motivates workers are achievable goals and rewards for those who meet or exceed them.

Understanding performance standards is essential in a cross-cultural environment because standards are the source of decision-makers' judgments about productivity, quality, and even personal character. Most individuals of one culture do not create standards against global benchmarks but rather against benchmarks of their own particular marketplace or culture. Therefore, when people from different cultures work together, they must define a shared meaning of excellence in order to come to a mutually acceptable set of performance standards. Once these standards are agreed upon, productivity, quality, and character can be measured more fairly and accurately, even across cultures. When objective standards are not applied, the tendency of workers will often be to attribute negative intent to decision-making managers. Such negative attributions result in discontent, declining morale, declining productivity, gossip, job dissatisfaction, and turnover—all costly consequences!

Even after differing standards are identified, however, conflicting opinions may arise about which to follow. If the standards emanate from different cultures, the need for cross-cultural analysis and interpretation becomes obvious. Even in a domestic organization, there will inevitably be management-worker confrontations if workers do not accept the standards by which they are evaluated. As the critical incident in this chapter makes clear, conflicts that revolve around differing performance standards can become very complicated indeed. The seemingly simple performance-review process can expand to include concerns about the fairness of evaluations and the reasonableness of goal setting and can result in lawsuits involving equal employment opportunity issues.

Step 1
Problem Identification

A. Statement of the Problem

A well-planned and well-executed performance-management system with clear standards plays a vital role in maintaining a motivated multinational workforce in a global organization. The planning and implementation of both standard-setting and performance-review systems that will gain wide acceptance in foreign subsidiaries are difficult tasks at best. One merely has to look at the great variety of performance-management systems and standards used in domestic companies to realize how challenging the task is. When employees from diverse national cultures work together in a single company, the job of defining and instituting equitable systems with clear standards becomes all the more difficult. The basic differences between how Japanese and American companies set standards, measure performance, and communicate the results to employees present unique difficulties in the effective motivation of employees. In addition, the complex and well-enforced American laws and accepted practices regarding equal employment opportunity often present a major challenge to Japanese managers who are unfamiliar with such practices. Although Japanese businesses are eager to comply with American laws, the differing standards by which women and minorities are judged in the two countries can be a source of friction and, potentially, legal action.

B. Description of the Incident

The Japanese president of an electronics subsidiary in the United States found himself in the unusual position of conducting formal performance reviews for his American department heads and vice president. Although he was not accustomed to being directly involved in reviews of such high-level employees, his American human resources manager had explained to him that American senior managers expect their superiors to give them yearly feedback in a formal setting. A fairly recent arrival in the United States, the Japanese president tried to learn as much as he could about American performance-review processes. Ultimately, he was able to construct what he thought was an effective mixture of American traditions and Japanese motivational techniques. This solution involved the combination of a one-page quantitative rating sheet of five comprehensive criteria and direct verbal feedback from the president himself. The Japanese president used his rating sheet to assess the American managers' performance in the areas of time, people, and project management, quality of leadership, and teamwork. In providing verbal feedback, the president concentrated on the areas in which his managers needed to improve.

In spite of his initial concerns, the president was quite satisfied with the meetings he had with all of his department heads. In addition to providing them with a formal evaluation and a motivational pep talk, especially toward the goals of improving customer service and reducing costs, he felt he had been successful in explaining to them the values and standards of the larger corporation. Upon initiating his final performance review, however, he could tell that his American vice president was very upset. As the review progressed, the American became more and more agitated, particularly when his suggestion to promote one of the female members of a key team in the salesforce to a management position was turned down. Near the end of their formal meeting, the president finally asked what was wrong. The American explained that all of his department heads had complained about their performance reviews. He said that the department heads were confused and upset and that they felt they had received unfairly negative evaluations. In addition, they expressed dissatisfaction with what they described as unrealistic customer service and cost reduction goals. Furthermore, the vice president told the Japanese president that he agreed with his department heads, particularly regarding goals which are impossible to attain. Finally, the American told the president that his failure to promote the outstanding female salesperson might very well lead her to sue the company for gender discrimination.

"The whole situation was a great surprise to me," the Japanese said.

> I am not used to having formal review meetings like this with my top managers, so I was very concerned when I learned that the Americans thought I was angry with them. I thought there must be a misunderstanding because my English

is not so good. Now I learn about all these other complaints, and I am very confused. I have always been successful at motivating my workers, and I used the same sort of goal-setting practices here that I have been using for years in Japan. After hearing the Americans complain about my expectations for customer service, I am beginning to think that they simply don't want to work very hard.

The prospect of legal trouble was also of great concern to the president. "I don't want our company to lose face over this issue," he said, "especially since we have worked so hard to conform to American laws. I even told the vice president that it was his responsibility to make sure that no legal situation arises."

The American managers had a very different perception of events. "We were all confused and angry after our performance reviews," one department head explained.

I mean, we all got five's on our written reports, which is the best you can do, and then we all got yelled at by the president during the personal feedback time. He had nothing but complaints! To make matters worse, when we asked for specific feedback about how to improve our performance, he said very loudly: "You should know what to do."

Others stressed his unrealistically high goals for customer service and cost reduction. "He kept telling us to call our customers every week," the American sales director said.

If I do that, my customers will think I'm trying to pester them to death. It's just like the goals he set for cost reduction; my salespeople were told they have to stay at cheap hotels on the edge of town when they travel. We can't even rent cars when we go to other cities—we have to take taxis. Also, I had told the president repeatedly that we needed to promote the most outstanding member of one of our sales teams—a woman—but he refused. To make matters worse, he hired a man from outside the company to fill the position I wanted her to have. If we keep this up, we're going to have a big problem on our hands.

Step 2
Problem Clarification

Intentions versus Perceptions

Intentions	
Japanese	**American**
• Help American workforce to do a better job by goal setting • Improve customer contact and control costs • Motivate the American workforce and follow American EEO guidelines	• Understand the mismatch between the written and oral evaluations • Handle customer service and cost control in the normal fashion • Motivate the salesforce and follow EEO guidelines

Perceptions	
Japanese	**American**
• Americans are too sensitive about receiving critical feedback • Americans are not used to working as hard as Japanese to strive toward high goals • The American vice president has bad judgment about when and whom to promote	• The Japanese president is lying about his opinions of us • There is no way to please the Japanese president • Japanese are sexists who don't want to promote women

Japanese Perspective

From his perspective, the Japanese president was doing his best to motivate his American workforce during their performance reviews.

> I can't understand why the Americans thought I was upset with them, since I was only trying to tell them how to be better in their jobs. After all, I made sure to give them all high marks on their written evaluations—I know that Americans need a lot of compliments in order to feel good about themselves. Maybe they are too sensitive about the whole thing. Japanese workers do not complain about being told how to improve, but Americans seem to have a problem with it. I don't know how I'm supposed to motivate them if they do not accept that there is always room for improvement. They demanded that I give specific examples of how they should improve. Why should I spoon-feed them? I think it is actually good to examine these issues oneself.

The president had similar intentions regarding setting goals for the subsidiary.

> I know the Americans are complaining that my expectations for customer service and cost reduction are too high. This sort of complaining is even worse than their confusion about their performance reviews. Everyone knows that workers are motivated when the company asks them to work toward very difficult goals—it is *joshiki* (common sense). If I set goals that are attainable, the workers would simply reach those goals and then stop working. Maybe Americans do not work so hard, but our subsidiary has to set high standards for customer service and cost control. If we do not hold down costs, headquarters will not continue to

support us. If we do not pay attention to our customers, we will not make any sales. Already I have heard complaints from the presidents of other Japanese subsidiaries that our salespeople are not contacting them often enough.

When it came to the issue of equal employment opportunity, the president intended to follow American legal guidelines. At the same time, he wanted to do what was best for the company.

I have to admit that I was shocked when the vice president suggested that we promote a woman from our best sales team into a management position. First of all, she has only been with the company two years; it is not yet time for her to be promoted. Also, it would be bad for morale if we broke up our most productive sales team by promoting her. To make matters worse, I know that she just got married. It would be bad timing to promote her right now, since she will probably leave the company to start having children soon. Since there wasn't a good candidate for the management position in our own company, I hired someone from the outside, as all American companies do. I don't want to have any legal trouble, but I still have to make decisions that will benefit the company.

American Perspective

The Americans had similar good intentions, but their perceptions varied considerably from those of the Japanese president. They were having difficulty understanding the apparent conflict between what the president had written about them and what he had said to them. One department head summed it up.

The president gave us a rating sheet that evaluated our performance on a scale from one to five in five different categories, one being the lowest score, five the highest. Not one of us got less than a four in any category, and no one got more than two fours. All the rest were fives. That seemed like pretty high praise, but when we got to the president's office, he yelled at us. I've never had a manager chew me out that way. I was in that office an hour, and he never said one positive thing about the way I was doing my job. He never even asked me a question. All the other department heads had the same experience. It's clear to us that the written reports are obvious lies—he was just sandbagging us so we couldn't complain to the company about his behavior.

When it came to goal setting, the Americans' intentions were to handle customer service and cost control in the same successful way they had in the past. The director of sales explained,

I've never seen anyone set such difficult goals when things were already going well. The president told me to direct my salespeople to be in contact with our customers on a weekly basis. That's ridiculous! When I asked him to explain what was wrong with our current customer service, he told me that the president of another U.S.-based Japanese company had complained about not seeing our salespeople often enough. He had never mentioned this incident to me before, and I couldn't believe he would bring up something so trivial. I don't think there's any way to satisfy him. Then when he set incredibly high goals for cost reduction, my salesforce was really unhappy. I had already made them pinch every penny they could, including the silly notion of staying at cheap hotels and taking taxis instead of rental cars. We set a record low for our expense account last year. Nevertheless, he told me that our performance still wasn't satisfactory because it hadn't met his goal. On the other hand, when his Japanese friends from headquarters came to visit, he put them up at the most expensive hotel in town and hired limousines to drive them around.

By urging the president to promote a female salesperson into management, the vice president intended to motivate his salesforce and to follow the company's policy of equal employment opportunity.

Everyone in the company knows who the most qualified member of our sales staff is, and it's only common sense to promote her. The rest of the salespeople need a role model to look up to, and she'll make them feel like they have a voice in the management of the company. When the president told me he wasn't going to promote her, I explained to him that she might take his rejection as a sign of gender discrimination. After all, she's the clear choice for the job. When I found out that the president's choice was a man from outside the company, I knew we had a problem. Now, I'm supposed to tell her that we can't promote her because she's going to start having children? Legally, we're not ever supposed to take her marital status into consideration, and I happen to know she and her husband aren't even interested in kids. I never wanted to believe all those stories about the Japanese being sexist, but I can't think of any other explanation for the president's actions.

Step 3
Cultural Exploration

Expectations and Assumptions

Japanese	American
• Top managers do not need to be given specific performance reviews	• Even top managers expect specific performance reviews and goals
• Workers are motivated by goals that are very difficult to achieve	• Workers are motivated by goals that are more readily attainable
• Customer service is based on developing lasting personal relationships through face-to-face contact	• Customer service is based on quality and price, not necessarily the number of times a salesperson visits the customer
• Married women are likely to leave the company and are therefore less appropriate candidates for promotion	• Employees must be promoted without regard to gender or marital status
• One should not single out a member of a team for reward or special attention	• Workers are motivated by role models who are drawn from their ranks and who receive special recognition

Japanese Perspective

Japanese companies have not traditionally had what Americans would think of as a formal performance-review system for managers. Executives were expected to motivate their subordinates by talking to them whenever they saw deficiencies. As time passed, however, Japanese companies started developing more formal evaluations, partly in an effort to comply with Japanese labor standards and partly as a reaction to American management practices that were taking hold around the world. Under this influence, Japanese performance reviews became more objective, with greater attention to measurable behavior.

Even with the use of more formal evaluation systems in Japan, however, it is unusual for the manager to discuss the evaluation scores directly with subordinates. Evaluations are typically sent directly to the human resources department for action.

The likely expectation of Japanese executives is that the people who report directly to them will already know their own deficiencies and will work to improve themselves. Detailed, behaviorally focused evaluations are an insult to older managers. Americans need to keep in mind that Japan has traditionally had a relatively homogeneous culture. People speak the same language, and they are used to living around and working with the same people all their lives. After spending so much time together, Japanese workers are able to predict or assume what their colleagues will think or feel about a certain situation. This feeling is represented in the concept of *ishin denshin* (tacit understanding, or "reading each other's heart").

The idea that the Japanese president would have to tell his own department heads how to do their jobs reinforced a common Japanese perception of Americans as lacking the maturity of an adult. One often hears Japanese talking in the bars and restaurants at night about how their American workers act like children—"they have to be told exactly what to do." They also speak of the United States as an "I Love You" culture, where workers are emotionally weak and need constant encouragement and words of exaggerated praise such as "great job" and "wonderful." Japanese executives respect managers who are able to attend to details without requiring instructions or compliments.

In a Japanese company, it is often the executive's responsibility to set goals. These goals may not need to be negotiated with labor if the company enjoys good labor-management relations. The expectation when a Japanese executive sets goals is that the workers will say "yes sir" and will work to achieve them. Arguing or debating with one's manager about an assigned goal is not acceptable. Since Japanese managers do not anticipate challenges to their orders, they often misinterpret as insubordination the approach Americans frequently take, which is to enter into a dialogue with their boss. If employees do not meet the assigned goals, they are usually expected to put their heads down and try harder. Goals may be set with the assumption that they will not be met for several years. Many Japanese do not accept the motivational theory that employees need to be able to reach goals and then pause to celebrate. It is common in the United States for Japanese executives to set goals and then push workers harder and harder to reach them. Some follow this process in Japan as well, especially older Japanese executives. It should be noted, however, that some Japanese companies set two goals—one "public" goal, which is given to the workers for motivational purposes, and a lower "private" goal, which is given to managers to let them know what is acceptable in the short term.

The Japanese standard of high expectations for workers is particularly strong when it comes to customer relations. Japanese companies value customers for the relationships they have with them, not just for the profit they bring, which is what drives customer relations in the United States. For the Japanese, appreciating your customers means being attentive to them. This implies frequent face-to-face contact, not just telephone calls or letters. From the Japanese perspective, if you are not in face-to-face contact with your customers, you are not putting yourself in the position of being in a relationship with them and you won't know their needs. In closely maintained relationships, however, you create a balance of opportunity and obligation, which enables you both to better understand your customers' circumstances and to anticipate more effectively their needs. Japanese companies expect to develop lifetime customers with whom they can demonstrate these competencies.

The Japanese model for personal relationships is the same as their model for customer relationships. Japan has long been a community-based culture where individuals expect to see the people who are important to them frequently. Japan has what Edward T. Hall, a well-known anthropologist, calls a high-context culture in which the meaning of what people do or say is significantly affected by the web of relationships they have and by nonverbal patterns of behavior. The fact that Japan has become more urban just means that people have to work harder to uphold the value of regular face-to-face communication. Still today, in Japan, the telephone is more an instrument for making appointments than for maintaining a business relationship. Even with the growth of e-mail, voice mail, and other impersonal forms of contact, nothing actually replaces face-to-face meetings, where the participants can get a better feel for what people need and for what their verbal communication really means.

When it comes to standards for promotion, the Japanese have traditionally valued experience first, then excellence. This reversal of the principle in production of "quality over quantity" is based on the belief that experience will result in quality over time. A worker is expected to spend a certain period of time at one level of the organization before being promoted to another. Managers also tend to value a worker's long-term commitment to the organization. If anything interferes with a manager's perceptions of a worker's loyalty, that worker may not be considered so valuable. These attitudes can—as in the case of the Japanese president in this chapter—cause Japanese managers to make promotion decisions that Americans would regard as sexist. The tendency of Japanese women to forsake work for motherhood leads Japanese managers to view married women as less loyal to the company. Although the role of women in Japanese society is changing, they still face many obstacles to advancement in Japanese companies. Societal pressures to look after one's family are particularly strong. So, after marriage and especially after children enter the picture, most Japanese women do leave their companies. This turns into a vicious cycle when companies, expecting women to leave, make few promotional opportunities available. The fact that workers are expected to spend a long time at low levels in the organization before being promoted keeps women from advancing through the ranks. Because of the lack of acceptable options to balance out their careers and personal obligations, many highly qualified and capable women have no choice but to leave their companies. In Japan, women who have babies and then put their children in child care are likely to be shunned unless they are single parents. Single parents sometimes live together in a kind of financial cooperative so that some may stay home with the children while others work. There is, however, a growing appreciation in Japan of the right of women to work and raise children at the same time.

American Perspective

In direct contrast to the Japanese experience, Americans are used to dealing with a diverse, heterogeneous workforce. There is no assurance that an individual will end up working with the same sort of people he or she grew up with, nor is there any guarantee that anyone will stay with the same company long enough to develop a strong relationship with upper management. Different ethnic backgrounds, religious beliefs, genders, regional peculiarities, even different languages—all these are common obstacles in the American workplace that keep workers from developing the sort of unspoken common understandings that Japanese workers take for granted. This makes for the converse of the high-context culture mentioned above: a low-context culture in which the context of relationships is more uncertain or more unstable and dependence on written and verbal communication to convey meaning is greater. As a result, most working Americans place great importance on receiving detailed performance reviews and instructions. After all, one cannot be sure exactly what the boss means when he or she says, "Do this better next time." For their part, American evaluators are used to providing detailed and objective evaluations—in a diverse workforce, it is believed that there is no other way to support the American value of equity among workers.

It is important to note, however, that top-level American managers often receive the same sort of nonspecific feedback top Japanese managers are used to giving. In a situation where experienced American managers have strong relationships with their superiors, you are not likely to find the sort of detail-oriented evaluations more common at lower levels of the company. That said, it might be expected that experienced American managers who are not used to receiving detailed performance reviews would have no problem dealing with a Japanese president who is not used to giving them. This is not the case. When confronted with what they perceive as an unknown style of management (that is, a Japanese style) with unknown standards of excellence, even experienced Americans, true to their low-context conditioning, will demand a great deal of direction, feedback, and support from their president. From the American perspective, it is important to ask for specific instructions when you are unfamiliar with your manager's expectations. Because they have sometimes had bad experiences that resulted from a misunderstanding with their supervisor, seasoned Americans would usually rather ask too many questions than too few. The standards for performance that the Japanese often regard as common sense and invariable, Americans regard as uncertain and unknown.

Another difference between American and Japanese standards lies in the contrast between the Japanese desire to engage in a continual pursuit of perfection (described in chapter 9 as *kaizen*) and the American tendency to believe that goals should be attainable and their achievement celebrated. This belief is related to the value Americans have traditionally placed on achievement, on action and "doing." Americans admire the person with a "can do" attitude. When a manager sets a goal, workers are expected to believe they can reach it, provided the goal is one that the manager honestly believes the workers can achieve in the near term. Americans do not value delayed gratification (evident in the behavior of American stockholders and the manner in which companies cater to them), which is one reason they tend to be perceived by the Japanese as immature. In modern times, these two expectations have caused management and labor to work increasingly toward a system where workers give input to managers, which then allows managers to set more realistic goals. It is not uncommon for individual employees to work with their managers to establish specific performance objectives. The American belief is that workers will be motivated if they are allowed to experience a continuous series of successes. It is also believed that workers who are never allowed to succeed will become discouraged. This is not to say, however, that American managers have low expectations. They believe that workers should have to put forth significant effort to meet their goals, but they also believe that those goals should be attainable. And, as said earlier, when goals are attained, Americans believe it is important to celebrate their accomplishment.

Statements similar to the following are often voiced by Americans who report to Japanese.

> I fully expect to have to stretch my own employees and resources to achieve new goals set by the Japanese. However, I also want a fighting chance to achieve those goals. The goals I'm given, however, merely set me up for failure. They are impossible to attain, so I never get the satisfaction of meeting, much less exceeding, the goals. Moreover, when I do report improved numbers, I'm not congratulated for the increase in production. Instead, my boss focuses on what I haven't achieved and severely chastises me. When he says that I "must" improve the output of my group, I feel like I am back in the military taking orders from a superior officer. As a manager with many years of

experience, I fully understand the importance of improving performance. I just wish they wouldn't order me about like a schoolboy. Why can't they at least recognize the tremendous accomplishments we have made, then calmly discuss strategies for further improvement?

Figure 1, below, illustrates the difference in goal-setting approaches more commonly taken by Japanese and Americans. The levels A through C can represent any type of goal, from production output to new accounts acquired. Level C is the highest level of accomplishment on this scale and is probably not attainable. Level A is the lowest. Given the position of the "current status," assume that none of these levels has ever been attained.

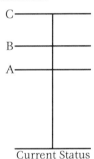

Current Status

Let's use this simple diagram to analyze three different goal-setting scenarios:

1. Japanese boss to Japanese subordinate

2. American boss to American subordinate

3. Japanese boss to American subordinate

Japanese boss to Japanese subordinate
Level-C goal set by Japanese boss

Japanese Manager's Intention	Japanese Subordinate's Reaction
• Must motivate employees to reach high • It is management's job to push subordinates to improve. Even if employees close in on goal (reach levels A or B), don't dwell on accomplish-ments. Continue to push for improvement by focusing on what still needs to be done	• Responds to directive with "Yes, I will do my best" • Might be continually thinking the goal is too high but will not complain or tell the manager that it can't be attained

In a situation such as this, the subordinate would not enter into a debate about the attainability of the goal during a meeting. In most cases, the subordinate would keep the manager informed of progress toward the goal during regular meetings. Those meetings may take place during office hours, but information of this type is, as has been stated previously, often shared after hours, at local restaurants or bars. It is during these many meetings that the subordinate can show how hard he and the team are working toward the goal. If progress is slow or if the goal seems too difficult, the boss will either give the employee more coaching or alter the goal slightly. An important point to remember is that a goal is altered only after the subordinate has already attempted to reach it, not through skilled debate when the assignment is initially made.

American boss to American subordinate
Level-B goal set by American boss

American Manager's Intention	American Subordinate's Reaction
• Must motivate employees to stretch. This is a high goal but realistic. A goal that is too high will be seen by employees as a prescription for failure	• "This goal is too high. Given the resources I have, I will never attain this. I must tell the manager two things: (1) why I can't reach this goal given my current resources and (2) what I need if he expects me to get there. If he doesn't give me any more resources, the best I can do is shoot for level A"

In this type of situation, it is not uncommon for the subordinate to respond immediately to the manager with a counterproposal. Assuming the subordinate can present an argument that is grounded in fact and experience, the manager may alter the goal (to somewhere between levels A and B) or provide the subordinate with more resources to achieve level B. During the initial meeting, the manager may still hesitate, telling the subordinate to "keep me posted on your progress," thereby delaying the decision to alter the goal.

Japanese boss to American subordinate
Level-C goal set by Japanese boss

Japanese Manager's Intention	American Subordinate's Reaction
• Must motivate employees to reach high. It is management's job to push subordinates continually to improve. Even if employees close in on a goal (reach levels A or B), don't dwell on accomplishments. Continue to push for improvement by focusing on what still needs to be done	• "This is impossible to attain. Setting unreasonable, idealistic goals is a demotivator. How am I expected to now go out and motivate my own American staff when I don't buy into the goals?"

This scenario usually ends up in frustration for both sides. The subordinate will likely voice objections to the manager during the meeting, often citing data or experience as a reason for not even attempting to reach level C goals. The American is fully expecting to enter into a dialogue with the manager in order to set a mutually agreeable, realistic goal. Instead, the manager, who is not accustomed to the subordinate pushing back, often responds with the order, "Don't give up without even trying. You must at least make an attempt." He feels that setting the goal any lower than level C would be too low and too easily attainable. Without striving for idealistic goals, new territory will never be uncovered; this is the essence of *kaizen*.

With respect to customer service, American salespeople operate with the knowledge that they will not necessarily enjoy much continuity with their customers over time. Unlike their Japanese counterparts, who can expect to have a lifelong relationship with many customers, Americans know that the highly mobile workforce will keep them moving from one customer to the next. Though a particular salesperson may serve the same company year after year, it is unlikely that the person or point of customer contact inside that company will remain the same. It is, therefore, difficult for Americans to develop or value long-term personal relationships with their customers. Instead, great value is placed on respecting the position held by a particular customer. A customer is treated with respect because he or she holds a particular position in relationship to the company, not because there is any history of a relationship with a specific salesperson. Because of this, Americans consider it appropriate to keep in touch with their customers using efficient, high-technology methods rather than face-to-face contact.

The movement to guarantee equal employment opportunities has a long history in the United States, and it is mandated by law that employers must treat their employees without regard to gender, ethnic background, age, marital status, or any other factor that is not directly related to workplace competence. Furthermore, there are a number of state and federal laws designed to provide legal support to those who have been discriminated against by their employers. For the most part, the only information employers are expected to consider when making decisions is how well a particular employee has performed his or her job. If there are other factors that affect a person's status in the organization, they must be objective, documented, agreed-upon considerations such as test scores, educational background, training, and so on. Diversity in the workforce is not merely something Americans are used to—they have come to place a great value on diversity as a source of innovation and creativity. Thus, it cannot be assumed that a woman who has recently married will leave the company to have children. The reality in America is that a woman in such a situation might have any one of a number of plans for the future, including placing her children in day care or choosing not to have children.

As far as promoting an outstanding member of a team is concerned, Americans believe that workers need to have role models whose success will motivate them to work harder.

Thus, it is considered appropriate to recognize outstanding team members by promotion as soon as their excellence is determined. The other team members will understand that hard work is rewarded. Americans expect their leaders to lead by moving up in the ranks of the organization to higher positions regardless of their gender, age, or seniority.

Step 4
Organizational Exploration

Global Imperatives

Local Conditions

Japanese	American
• Americans aren't aware of the big picture outside the United States, so some decisions will be top-down • Because the electronics industry is fast-moving, even more emphasis must be placed on customer service • Cost control is particularly important for a struggling subsidiary • This is a new area of confusion for management; knowledge of EEO doesn't guarantee appropriate action	• Executives have a right to take part in the goal-setting process, especially if difficult goals are going to be announced • Customer service is of primary importance because we cannot take loyalty for granted • The cost controls were too harsh and relatively ineffective. They were for "show" only • The Japanese need to rely upon local managers and trainers for EEO guidance

Japanese Perspective (Global Imperatives)

In conducting his performance reviews, the Japanese president in this chapter was influenced by a number of organizational imperatives imposed upon him either directly or indirectly by headquarters. In his experience, it was normal not to give high-level managers very specific feedback. This tendency on his part was strengthened by the fact that he was in an unfamiliar situation with unfamiliar department heads. When confronted by the unknown, Japanese managers tend to become more reserved because of the value they place on *enryo,* or hesitation. *Enryo* is the value of holding back or being reserved and not really letting one's true feelings be known in the interest of keeping some semblance of harmony in the group. Even Americans exhibit this value, yet not nearly as much as the Japanese. Hence, the president intended to keep his comments in the feedback sessions relatively general. He was also influenced by the Japanese high-context communication style discussed earlier, that is, "They should already know, why go into the details."

The standards of the headquarters organization also influenced the Japanese president's decisions regarding goal setting in the areas of customer service and cost reduction. The electronics industry is fast-moving, and customers' needs change rapidly. From the perspective of the headquarters organization, this meant that even greater emphasis should have been placed on customer relations. The president's tendency to stress customer relations was intensified by the pressure he was getting from his superiors in Japan to create a salesforce that could keep up with American customers' needs. A similar imperative affected his decisions regarding cost control. Because the subsidiary was relatively new and revenue was not yet significant, there was great pressure on the president to stress cost control as a method of keeping the subsidiary from operating at a loss. The specific method of cost control he established—mandating a change in the quality of hotels and a ban on automobile rentals for the salesforce—was also clearly the result of headquarters' influence. In Japan, where quality public transportation is abundant and hotels are located close to metropolitan centers, these sorts of cost reduction strategies make sense. It is, however, important to note that cost control standards were not considered to be universally applicable by the headquarters organization; while it was deemed appropriate for the salesforce to stay in second-tier hotel chains, headquarters would not have been happy had visiting Japanese executives received the same treatment. As with performance reviews, a different set of standards applied to those at the highest levels of management.

The issue of equal employment opportunity (EEO) and how to work with the promotion of women into more senior management positions is relatively new to the Japanese. Of course, many corporations in Japan are hiring women college graduates into career-track and professional positions. However, there are still relatively few women managers in the large Japanese corporations in Japan. Japanese women have actually made much more progress in the foreign corporations located in Japan. Hence, even though he received some training on EEO issues prior to departure, the president wasn't thinking of how his decision to promote an external candidate, a man, instead of the woman from inside the company would appear to be a gender-driven decision. A more thorough analysis of this topic appears on pages 164-68 at the end of this chapter.

American Perspective (Local Conditions)

Like the Japanese president, the American executives were being influenced by the standards of a larger context—in their case, the local workplace. The most significant of these influences was in the area of goal setting. There were a number of cultural factors that caused the Americans to react negatively to the Japanese president's emphasis on customer relations and cost control, but there were also significant local conditions that contributed to their negative reaction, specifically, the belief that executives have the right to take part in the goal-setting process. In a sales-oriented organization, it is considered important for top managers (as well as union representatives, in some cases) to have quarterly or yearly meetings with the president to discuss corporate goals. These meetings are expected to be serious and substantive because the input of the vice president and department heads is seen as an indispensable resource for the president to use in making final decisions. For the president to set what seemed to the Americans to be unusually high or aggressive goals without seeking their input appeared to be an unwarranted slap in the face. "Common sense" mandates the participation of executives in goal setting because department heads have valuable knowledge about the local marketplace. When the president set goals without attempting to access their knowledge, the Americans felt that he was foolish, inconsiderate, and irresponsible.

As explained earlier, the hierarchical nature of Japanese society and Japanese corporations drives the notion that the boss is the leader and the subordinate watches and obeys. This flies in the face of local conditions, which call for a more open dialogue between manager and subordinate. The thought of being outside the information or power loop, particularly for Americans who have previously worked in American corporations as managers or executives, is enough to cause some to look for new jobs.

Step 5
Conflict Resolution

Complex conflicts such as the ones discussed in this chapter are not often solved with a single sweeping action. This incident involves five issues that frequently cause trouble for Japanese and Americans working together:

1. performance reviews

2. goal setting and motivation

3. customer relations

4. cost containment

5. equal employment opportunity issues

This section will address how each of these issues was resolved through a combination of education, discussion, and negotiation.

The first step on the road to achieving harmony involved a series of training workshops about Japanese business practices for American representatives from the various departments. Participants included the vice president and the department heads, plus additional members of each department. This program was designed to help the Americans understand the cultural and organizational underpinnings of their Japanese president's approach to performance reviews, goal setting, and equal employment opportunity practices. The Japanese president sent his Japanese executives to these training sessions in order to learn more about the concerns of Americans and to help explain the Japanese perspective. As a result, both the American managers and the Japanese executives became involved in the process of conflict resolution. The president himself participated in several key discussions. By the end of the program, the Americans were able to define and clarify their problems with Japanese practices, and they understood better the cultural and organizational factors at work in the conflicts that were occurring. In addition the president and other Japanese executives began to understand the differences between American and Japanese standards. Finally, the outside consultants who had been brought in to assist in resolving the conflicts and who served as cultural mediators during the training sessions were able to attain a deeper understanding of the issues and develop a practical approach to resolving them.

Nevertheless, although the Americans now understood why their Japanese president had conducted his performance reviews in the way he had, they were not satisfied. Similarly, their desire to be involved in the goal-setting process was not lessened by their understanding of how goals were normally set in the corporate culture of their Japanese parent company. These two conflicts required quite a lot of time and effort to resolve. A group of managers decided to approach the task by setting up bicultural task forces. All task force members had to have attended the training workshop so that they shared an understanding of the cultural and organizational foundations of the problems they were confronting. The first task force was set up to resolve the performance-review conflict.

Performance Reviews

In the meetings of the task force on performance reviews the president explained that, even though he would like to provide effective feedback to his department heads and vice president in Japan, it was unusual for department heads to need detailed, objective feedback in a formal setting and that he was not used to conducting formal reviews in this fashion. The Americans pointed out that such reviews were a normal American business practice. In the end, the president agreed that they were appropriate, especially in the United States, where they could protect a company from frivolous lawsuits, but he still had difficulty doing them for senior staff. At this point the Americans conceded that high-level American executives, like their Japanese counterparts, also do not normally have formal review sessions with their top American managers. But when the president is from another culture and operates by standards unfamiliar to them, they do need more specific information about how they are performing and what is expected of them. Since the Japanese president felt he had communicated his standards clearly, this led to a discussion about just how specific standards have to be for Americans. After it was made clear that the Americans were more concerned with understanding their president's standards and expectations than with the particular format of their performance reviews, both sides were able to reach a compromise.

First, it was agreed that a system of detailed, objective job descriptions and performance reviews would be established for all of the employees except for the senior staff. Second, the president agreed to give a presentation about his five guiding principles for the organization at an informal dinner with the senior staff. Third, each of the Americans agreed to have individual meetings with the president to discuss how his five principles applied to their particular departments. Finally, they all agreed to a new system of senior staff performance reviews which would be a blend of Japanese and American styles. The Japanese president would give monthly, informal verbal feedback to his managers throughout the course of the year, which might even occur off-site.[1] In a more typical American style, the president agreed to give annual performance reviews that focused on each manager's progress and anticipated career directions. For their part, the Americans would request, without becoming defensive, specific suggestions as to ways in which they could improve. Both the American managers and their Japanese president were happy with this compromise and agreed to implement it immediately.

Finally, the president agreed to undergo some individual tutoring on how to effectively give feedback to his American managers.

Goal Setting

The American managers explained that they wanted to be involved in the goal-setting process. The Japanese managers believed such decision-making power should reside only with the president. The Americans made it clear, however, that American presidents are not required to set goals at the exact levels their managers want. Instead, department heads contribute information and make recommendations, and the president has final say. With this point clarified, the Japanese president agreed to hold formal goal-setting sessions where his vice president and department heads could supply information and make recommendations regarding goals, while the Americans agreed to respect the final decision of the president.

---

[1] See chapter 10 for a fuller discussion of the issues that arise out of different styles of giving feedback.

The goal-setting task force also addressed the issue of how high the goals should be set. The Americans explained that their workers needed to have more achievable goals to be effectively motivated. The Japanese described their traditional method of setting very difficult goals in order to keep workers focused on achievement. The American participants said Americans are used to working even after goals have been reached, especially if they can expect some sort of compensation or recognition for such overachievement. Further discussion revealed that Japanese companies are not as rigid on this issue as they seem and often have both a public and a private set of goals. The public or "idealistic" goals are very difficult if not impossible to reach, while the private or "realistic" goals are lower and more easily attainable. It was also pointed out that American companies with subsidiaries in Japan had found it necessary to adopt the Japanese two-goal system in order to motivate workers—an ideal goal for their Japanese workers and a realistic one for headquarters in the United States. This struck everyone as a good idea. It was decided that they would do the same thing in reverse relative to global/local perspectives, that is, establish high goals for headquarters in Japan while giving their American workers a midrange goal. The president agreed to institute performance-based bonuses to ensure that their workers were consistently motivated. However, he assured his managers that none of this meant he would expect them to work less than before.

The remaining three issues (customer relations, cost containment, and equal employment opportunity) were more readily resolved through creative problem-solving strategies.

Customer Relations

Understanding that the president's emphasis on face-to-face customer contacts meant having the salesforce maintain a relationship with the Japanese presidents of their corporate customers, the Americans were able to devise a plan to satisfy both the president and the salespeople. Instead of requiring the salespeople to meet face-to-face with their customers' American purchasing agents, which would have seemed excessive to the American purchasing agents, they would arrange frequent "relationship-building" meetings between their salespeople and their customers' top-level Japanese managers. These meetings would be for the purpose of maintaining relationships rather than producing sales. This would allow them to attend both to the long-term relationships the Japanese desired and the more efficient communication style the American purchasing agents were comfortable with.

Cost Containment

The problem involving the Japanese president's cost-control measures became a model for achieving intercultural effectiveness and came about in the following manner. The Americans understood why the president had instituted these measures, but they also felt that the new requirements were producing very little actual savings while exacting a high cost in morale. The Americans felt that the expense of cab fare from the outlying hotels they were being asked to stay in added so much travel cost that it outweighed any savings gained. They also claimed that the lack of accessibility created by the requirement that they stay in outlying hotels hurt their ability to make sales and build relationships. To assist in persuading the president to change his policy, they compiled statistical data which demonstrated its higher cost. At this juncture, however, they were advised to consider a more culturally appropriate approach to the president than directly presenting him with the facts and proving him wrong. They began instead by asking some of the lower-level Japanese managers in the company for guidance. The Japanese were very responsive and became "culture coaches." They started out describing to the Americans the traditional Japanese preference for using third-party mediators when dealing with delicate matters like establishing new relationships or resolving conflict. This approach allows the two parties with a vested interest in the outcome to maintain harmony, establish or maintain a good relationship, and, most important where conflict is involved, save face.

A key point the Americans learned from their Japanese counterparts was that regardless of how compelling their facts were, if they were not presented to the president in a manner that allowed him to save face, he would probably dismiss them outright. It was suggested that the Americans let the Japanese communicate the proposal to the president first, which would front-load him with the information so that he would not be surprised when they presented their findings. As is often the case, the Japanese handled this touchy matter after work hours, over drinks at the local restaurant. This culturally sensitive approach produced results. Since the data were compelling, the president agreed to change the travel policy but saved face by doing it without publicly or formally having been proven wrong. It was truly a win-win solution.

Equal Employment Opportunity

Although not as complex as the conflicts involving performance reviews and participation in goal setting, the equal employment opportunity issue had to be dealt with in a more comprehensive fashion. In this case, it was decided that a meeting between the president and the American vice president was required. During the meeting, the president expressed concern about the female candidate's ability to manage others. "As an individual contributor, she has an outstanding record in sales. Unfortunately, she has no experience as a manager and this is a source of great concern. I need a proven leader in that position, not just an outstanding salesperson." With that explanation of the requirements of the position, the American was able to accept the president's decision not to promote her. He agreed that she could use more time honing her leadership skills. He was, however, very clear in stating that the other, cultural reasons for not promoting her were illegal in the United States and could not be allowed to influence business decisions.

With these issues cleared up, the vice president set about trying to figure out a compromise he felt would be fair, legal, and acceptable to all parties. The idea he came up with was this: instead of immediately promoting her into a formal management position, the company would create a new position, "team leader," and appoint her to it. As team leader, she would have some supervisory responsibility over other team members and would receive an increase in salary and benefits, all of which would be a clear signal to her that she was moving up the management ranks.

Before presenting his idea to the president, he wisely decided to consult the Japanese culture coaches who had been so helpful in devising a strategy to deal with the travel expense issue. Their assistance this time came in the form of a thorough briefing on the cultural and organizational reasons why the president had reacted the way he did and on the substantial differences between American and Japanese perspectives on women in the workforce.

They emphasized the importance of couching his presentation to the president in terms of these differences so the proposal could be understood in terms of its appropriateness in the American context. They also suggested that after reminding the president that he had been given the job of avoiding legal action, the vice president should explain that Americans are motivated by outstanding role models who rise from their ranks into supervisory positions. In addition, American women, unlike the Japanese, do not as commonly have children immediately after marriage; and even if they do, they are more likely to continue working. Federal laws, in fact, protect the right of women to return to their jobs after taking a short maternity leave.

Finally, the vice president presented his proposal. He emphasized that promoting the female salesperson to the position of team leader would both motivate the other salespeople and give the new team leader the opportunity to prove her abilities as a manager. For his part, the Japanese president was surprised to discover that American workers are pleased when one of their rank is promoted ahead of the rest. The concept of promoting positive, outstanding role models in the salesforce was new to him, but he was intrigued at the prospect of using American management techniques to improve productivity. At the end of their meeting, the president approved his American vice president's proposal.

Step 6
Impact Assessment

Implementation of the new plans for goal setting and customer relations was overseen by the vice president, while the human resources manager supervised the new performance review and equal employment opportunity plans. After observing the entire goal-setting process and eliciting reports from each of the department heads, the vice president concluded that the workforce as a whole felt a greater commitment to the company's goals than they had in the past. Workers not only felt they could achieve their new goals but also that they had a greater voice in the goal-setting process. A similar increase in satisfaction took place in the area of customer relations. The president, in particular, expressed his satisfaction that more of his Japanese counterparts were happy with the amount of attention they were receiving from the salesforce, while the salespeople were happy about the reversal of the travel policy.

Realizing that some of the problems illustrated in this chapter were brought to light by needs assessment interviews, the human resources manager decided to conduct an annual employee satisfaction survey, including questions regarding performance reviews and gender equity. She found the employees happier with the new performance-review process and job descriptions but still received complaints of gender discrimination. Two actions were taken. First, the written standards were strengthened. Second, a training program was set up for both Japanese managers and American workers to increase knowledge and skills in communicating about gender equity issues. As Japanese managers became more skillful in talking about the differences between Japanese and American standards for working women and as more Americans learned how to talk to their Japanese superiors about discrimination concerns, there were fewer complaints in the annual satisfaction survey.

As a result of the new standards for performance management, the company experienced a number of benefits. The new worker commitment to productivity goals set by management decreased turnover and increased production. As workers participated in the goal-setting process and came to share the standards set by their organization, their feeling of involvement and commitment inspired them to work harder to achieve goals. Just the feeling that the goals were attainable raised morale, but workers were also motivated to strive for the bonuses given to those who surpassed the goals. The new customer relations standards resulted in a better relationship between the company's president and his Japanese counterparts, and the new travel policy made the salespeople happier, who were able to spend more time with customers and increase sales.

The sales team over which the woman was appointed leader established itself as the most effective in the organization, and the company's demonstrated commitment to gender equity reduced tension between Japanese management and American workers, increased communication around key issues, and allowed better relationships to develop. The rest of the workforce was also pleased with the new performance-review process, and, overall, company morale improved.

Step 7
Organizational Integration

The accomplishments of the conflict resolution process were reported in full in the corporate newsletter. As a part of the overall plan for implementing more formal performance-review processes, the human resources office developed documentation for job descriptions and for the performance reviews themselves. The vice president and the president worked out the new process for setting corporate goals and the president periodically met with the sales managers to report on the comments given to him by his Japanese counterparts in customer companies.

In addition to a *bonenkai*, an end-of-the-year celebration involving the president and the senior staff, each department manager initiated a *bonenkai* of his own to recognize the department's achievements. These involved many toasts and other celebrations, and in sales it was used as an opportunity for the Americans to ask their Japanese coworkers for advice on how best to deal with their Japanese customers during the coming year. The sales department manager also took the opportunity at his *bonenkai* to celebrate the new team leader's promotion.

Further integration of the outcomes of the conflict resolution was achieved by drawing the Japanese managers into the goal-setting process. These managers are expatriates generally unfamiliar with the American marketplace, and this unfamiliarity hinders the realization of their full potential during their service in the United States. The assumption is that the Japanese will pick up knowledge of the local marketplace by reading American newspapers and trade journals and by making use of the training they received in Japan. However, because many Japanese workers do not have sufficient English language skills, they choose to read Japanese publications instead. As a result, they are not up-to-date on the changing characteristics of the American marketplace. By including the Japanese staff in the goal-setting process, the company gave them the opportunity to learn more about the local marketplace from their American colleagues. If the Japanese had not participated, they would not have been as committed to the new goals, nor would they have understood how those goals were being communicated to headquarters.

Legal Aspects of Gender and Race Relations in the American Workplace

The purpose of this section is to emphasize the importance for Japanese expatriates in U.S.-based subsidiaries to be thoroughly informed about three critical areas: equal employment opportunity, affirmative action, and sexual harassment. The authors of this book have seen the negative consequences of business decisions made by many Japanese managers who were not sufficiently prepared to deal with the laws protecting the rights of American employees. Lawsuits resulting from the failure of Japanese companies to work effectively within the legal parameters found in these three areas have been front-page news in the U.S. media. In the preceding chapters, we have pointed out the consequences facing Japanese employers and American employees should they fail to work effectively across cultures. In most cases, those consequences were disgruntled employees, low productivity, or high turnover—certainly troublesome but not likely to wind up in highly publicized lawsuits.

In contrast, we have discussed in this chapter a potential incident of discrimination which resulted from a Japanese manager's assessment of the ability of his female subordinate based partly upon her gender, as well as on her abilities as a leader of a sales team. This section examines three other gender- and race-related issues which, if not appropriately dealt with, can result in extremely volatile, highly visible, and potentially crippling lawsuits that can damage a company from both a public relations and an economic standpoint. This is not intended as a legal guide. The authors strongly suggest that all questions the reader may have about legal issues be directed to their human resources or legal departments, especially now that Supreme Court decisions are reversing many affirmative action laws of recent decades.

The incidents below are provided for two main reasons: (1) to illustrate the variety of ways in which Japanese companies in the United States can find themselves in trouble and (2) to motivate the reader to assess the state of EEO awareness in his or her company and possibly implement some of the strategies we suggest.

All three of the incidents actually occurred in U.S.-based Japanese companies. Sadly, variations of these incidents occur all too frequently, and, with the increasing number of Japanese expatriate managers managing Americans, the odds are great that the number will increase even more. After examining these situations, it would be beneficial for Japanese and American personnel to discuss both the problems presented in each incident and what their company is doing to protect itself from making similar mistakes. The conflict resolution model introduced in chapter 2, particularly the Key Issue Worksheet, can be used to format the discussions. Through systematic joint consideration of these complex issues, Japanese and American managers can come to a fuller understanding of their intricacies. Effective strategies to eliminate illegal practices can be determined only after these issues, especially the cultural factors, are thoroughly understood by both sides.

Critical Incident 1

A Japanese manager who has been in the United States for four years introduces a newly arrived Japanese engineer to the American staff. When he introduces the new man to a woman who is a staff engineer, the manager says, "I'd like to introduce you to Karen. She is a good engineer who will work with you on the project." Then he adds, "By the way, Karen is single."

The two men laugh. Several days later, the director of the employee relations division informs the Japanese manager that Karen has filed a complaint of sexual harassment. When filing the complaint, Karen observed that it was no wonder women never got promotions to upper management in Japanese companies, since the Japanese only looked at women as sex objects and were "always joking about women." Whether Karen's complaint of sexual harassment will be upheld in a court of law is not the question. The point is that an ugly environment was being created by unwelcome comments and the Japanese had no idea that anything they were saying was wrong. Based on the training the Japanese had received in Japan, they were under the impression that as long as they didn't ask for sexual favors, base promotions upon receipt of sexual favors, or grab their female staff, there would be no problems. Given proper training, the Japanese could have avoided this type of incident, as well as the serious employee relations difficulties which resulted.

Critical Incident 2

One Japanese company with the best of intentions decided to sponsor a seminar on sexual harassment. The primary audience for the seminar was to be the Japanese expatriates who staffed the company's U.S.-based subsidiaries. The objective was to inform the expatriates about the issues surrounding sexual harassment in the American workplace and to help them avoid the many common legal problems related to them. The Japanese sponsors at headquarters sent out small flyers to its American subsidiaries in order to advertise the event. In addition to describing the content of the seminar, the flyer contained a Japanese-style cartoon (*manga*) of a man touching a woman's breasts. In Japan, cartoons are not taken seriously, and it is common practice to use them to portray sexual situations. From a Japanese point of view, one cartoon is the same as any other, whether or not it contains sexual content. In the United States, however, less distinction is made between whether an image is portrayed realistically or in a cartoon—many Americans consider overt sexual imagery of any kind to be offensive. Thus, even though the drawing was done in a cartoonlike manner and the intention of the company was good, American employees at the U.S. subsidiary were deeply offended by the flyer. This supposedly well-informed Japanese company was actually perpetuating the harassment problem by distributing material which could be viewed as offensive. The president of the company promoting the seminar was shocked when informed that "such a silly cartoon" had been viewed as a form of harassment. Thus the Japanese, while intending to do something constructive and positive, created the very problem they wished to avoid.

Critical Incident 3

A Japanese manager is part of a team interviewing new college graduates for engineering positions. The only criteria required were a good grade point average and some practical skills. The Japanese rejected a black male applicant. When asked the reason why, the manager stated that the applicant's hands were too large. His rationale was that because of his large hands, the applicant probably would not be able to perform some calibrations on machinery which required "fine motor skills." The manager was in favor of hiring an Asian applicant with smaller hands. He was told by the American members of the hiring team that his rationale didn't make any sense because there were other engineers on staff who had equally large hands and who performed the tasks with great precision and that hand size was not a legal criterion for rejection. It appeared to the Americans that the Japanese was consciously or unconsciously favoring the Asian applicant because of his race. The Japanese manager couldn't understand why the Americans were so concerned with his decision and refused to change it. The black applicant was not offered a job, which left the company in a very dangerous position.

These three incidents clearly illustrate a fact of life in the United States: sexual harassment and discrimination issues are often subtle and difficult to understand, even for American managers. American corporations have spent large sums of money both to train employees about these issues and to pay legal fees when laws were broken. So, it should be no surprise to discover that when expatriates come to this country, many are confused and angered by some of the laws and by the lawsuits that follow when laws are broken. This is especially true for Japanese expatriates, who come from an environment traditionally unconcerned with equality of the sexes.

One part of the solution to this problem is the better preparation of Japanese personnel assigned to U.S. subsidiaries. Japanese managers and trainers in Japan need to reexamine with great care the content of their predeparture orientation to assure that personnel being sent to the United States understand the legal strictures related to race and gender relations in the American workplace.

8

Operational Systems

Case Study: Information Management and Decision Making

The transformation of market information and performance standards into organizational behavior that achieves the strategic goals of the business is vital. This requires building *operational systems* in the subsidiary, the most important of which are the decision-making system and the information management system that supports it. Unfortunately, many U.S.-based Japanese subsidiaries are poorly prepared to make timely, strategic decisions that fit the U.S. market. Moreover, once decisions are made, the ability to transfer information effectively to the proper people and ensure appropriate action is severely handicapped by cultural differences.

There are many reasons for this, yet two stand out as primary culprits in the breakdown of the information-sharing system. First, many of the Japanese who manage U.S. subsidiaries come with the presumption that there is no other system than the "natural" one, which is based on "common sense," which governs operations in Japan at headquarters, and which everyone is expected to follow. Second, Americans assume that their system is the normal one. It happens often in any business milieu. Americans in positions of leadership often go from one American company to another with a presumption that certain systems they have used in the past at other companies are the most effective, and they proceed to implement them without educating anyone as to why they are better. Similarly, Japanese managers bring systems from Japan without accounting for the differing expectations of their American employees. In short, every organization embodies a set of perceptions, even within the same country, about how to operate that differs—sometimes slightly, sometimes greatly—from that of every other organization. It is important to make sure that information-sharing processes are designed to surmount obstacles raised by those differences.

In any organization, those who make important decisions rely on the smooth operation of information management systems. Organizational assumptions about information management influence standards regarding information sharing, for example, who shares what with whom, when, where, and how. Japanese organizations, for example, tend to have "nice to know" information-sharing systems, where information is widely disseminated. American organizations, on the other hand, tend to have "need to know" systems, where information is shared more selectively. In an American system, managers decide whether they need to share each item of information with their employees, while the employees like to assess whether the boss has made a good decision based on all the information they have. Informed decision making from the American point of view means that everyone knows what he or she needs to know in order to make appropriate judgments and take effective action.

The Japanese agree, but also believe that information is a means of motivation toward teamwork, loyalty, and commitment to the company. In Japan managers sometimes share information in order to generate positive attitudes, such as sharing bad news about the company's financial situation in order to generate motivation to work harder on the part of the employees. Unfortunately, in U.S.-based Japanese organizations many Americans report they feel "out of the information loop." This is curious, given that it suggests the Japanese are withholding information, which is in stark contrast to the wide dissemination of information in the "nice to know" approach they typically take in Japan. This chapter will examine why the smooth flow of information, so vital to timely, effective decision making, is such a problem for Japanese subsidiaries in the United States. (Note: American subsidiaries in Japan have exactly the same problem in reverse.)

Step 1
Problem Identification

A. Statement of the Problem

Cross-culturally inappropriate assumptions about the most effective way to share information and make decisions lead to many frustrating interactions between American and Japanese employees. If the obvious challenge of language difference was removed, there would still be many culturally driven differences that would and do lead to miscommunication, mistrust, and lost business opportunities. American and Japanese perceptions differ greatly on how to approach such issues as deciding who should get what type of information; what kind of information is proper to discuss publicly; the correct way to lead and participate in meetings; whether to communicate in person, by memo, e-mail, or telephone; how to make requests for information; and how to get fellow workers to "buy in" to ensure follow-through on tasks.

Misunderstandings that result from different approaches to these issues lead to frustration and cultural conflict among Japanese and Americans. Confusion arises as to the kind and quality of information needed and the amount of time required to process that information at headquarters or in the subsidiary. Disagreements occur over the who, what, why, how, when, and where of information sharing. Conflicts erupt because of misunderstandings about the relative importance of face-to-face interaction. Differing expectations about the priority of personal relationships or task accomplishment influence the timing and context of information sharing. Some of these problems can even be found in companies where there is no interaction between people from different cultures. Still, they are all made more complex by cultural differences. Americans and Japanese who accept this and work together to overcome their differences will succeed.

B. Description of the Incident

An American sales manager of a large Japanese manufacturing company in the United States sold a multimillion-dollar order to an American customer. This order was to be sourced from Japan. As part of the sales agreement, the customer requested that some changes be made in the specifications of the standard product. The customer expected the changes to be made and the order to be delivered within a specified time period. Since the company had never made a sale to this American customer before, the sales manager was eager to provide good service and a quick response time. To ensure a coordinated effort, she organized a strategic planning session of the managers from the key divisions that would be involved in processing the order. She sent copies of the agenda for the meeting to each participant. In addition to the sales manager and four other Americans, three Japanese managers attended: the heads of finance and customer support and the Japanese liaison to manufacturing at headquarters. The three Japanese managers had each been in the United States for less than two years.

The strategic planning meeting was scheduled to last one hour, and the sales manager planned to include a brainstorming session to discuss strategies for dealing with the customer's request, a discussion of possible time lines, and the next steps each manager would take. The American managers dominated the meeting by actively participating in the brainstorming session and the discussions that ensued. They proposed a preliminary time line and an initial action plan. The Japanese managers contributed very little during the brainstorming session, although they did talk to each other in Japanese. When the sales manager asked them for their opinion about the Americans' proposed action plan, two of the Japanese managers said they needed more time to think about it. The other looked down at the table, sucked air through his teeth, and said, "It may be difficult in Japan."

Concerned about the lack of Japanese participation in the meeting but eager to process the customer's order in a timely manner, the sales manager sent an e-mail to those who had attended the meeting. It contained a written version of the proposal the American managers had made and asked each person to give his or her reactions to it. The sales manager stated frankly that some of the managers had not participated very much in the meeting, but she was also very clear about the need for timely action. If she did not receive any further contributions from the managers within a week, she would assume consensus and follow the recommended actions of the American managers. The e-mail was sent, and a week passed without any further input from the Japanese managers. Satisfied that she had reached consensus on this subject, the American sales manager proceeded with the proposed time line and action plan, which called for sending the specifications and the requested delivery deadline by e-mail to headquarters in Tokyo, requesting that priority attention be given to the order. After a week, without any response from Tokyo, she sent another e-mail asking for a confirmation of the ability of headquarters to fill the order. The reply came the next day: "Thank you for the proposal. We are currently considering your request." Time passed, while the customer repeatedly asked about the status of the order. The only response she could give was that there was no information yet. Concerned, she sent yet another e-mail to Tokyo in which she outlined the specifications and time line as requested by the customer. She also reminded her contact of the potential size of the order and wrote that the deal might fall through if she didn't receive confirmation immediately. In addition, she asked the Japanese liaison to headquarters manufacturing to see if he could determine the cause of the delay. Three days later, the liaison told her that there was some resistance to the proposal and that it would be difficult to meet the deadline.

The customer, when informed, gave her a one-week extension but said they were also talking with another vendor and would take their business elsewhere if she didn't produce immediate results. Frantic, she again asked the Japanese liaison to intercede. Her bonus for the year and her division's profit margin rested on the success of this sale. As before, she was told that it would be difficult to meet the customer's demands so quickly and that the sales manager should please ask the customer to be patient. She did, and they lost the contract.

Infuriated, the American sales manager went directly to her Japanese president, explained what had happened, and complained about the lack of commitment displayed by both her contacts at headquarters and her Japanese colleagues here in the United States. The president told her that although he shared her disappointment in losing the contract, there were things she did not understand about the subsidiary's relationship with headquarters. The Japanese liaison had informed him that headquarters refused her order because it had already committed the majority of its output for the next few months to a customer in Japan. In a rage, the sales manager asked the president how she was supposed to attract customers when it was clear that the Americans in the subsidiary were getting no support from the Japanese and were being treated like second-class citizens by headquarters. Why, she asked, wasn't she told that Tokyo was committed to other customers?

"The Japanese are too slow in making decisions," the American sales manager said.

> By the time they get everyone on board in Japan, the U.S. customer has already gone shopping elsewhere. They are so secretive with their information. This whole mess started because they don't participate in our meetings. We invite them and then they just sit and talk to each other in Japanese. Are they hiding something from us? I never know what they're thinking, and it drives me crazy when they say things like "It is difficult" or when they suck air through their teeth. It doesn't help that they never respond to my written messages. Don't these guys ever read their memos? I sent that memo out immediately after the meeting so they would have plenty of time to react. I wonder if they are really committed to our sales mission or if they are putting me off. They seem more concerned about how we interact when we're trying to solve the problem than they do about actually solving it. There's clearly some sort of Japanese information network that I'm not a part of. I feel as if I work in a vacuum, and it makes me look foolish to the customer. They're too confident in the superiority of their product over the competition and too conservative to react swiftly to the needs of the market here. I know that headquarters in Tokyo reacts much more quickly to similar requests from their big customers in Japan, so it makes me and our customers feel as if we are not a very important market...like a forgotten stepchild.

"The American salesforce is too impatient," the U.S.-based Japanese managers said.

> They treat everything as though it is an emergency, and they never plan ahead. They call

meetings at the last minute and expect people to come ready to solve a problem about which we know nothing in advance. It doesn't really seem as if they want our feedback at all, since they speak so rapidly and use so much slang. By the time we understood what they were talking about in the meeting, they were off on a different subject, so we gave up trying to participate. The meeting leader said something about time lines or deadlines, but we weren't sure what she wanted, so we just agreed by saying yes so as not to hold up the meeting. How can they expect us to be serious about participating in their brainstorming session? Brainstorming is nothing more than guessing in public—it is irresponsible.

The Americans also rely too much on written communication. They send us too many memos and too much e-mail. They seem content to sit in their offices creating a lot of paperwork without knowing how people will react. They are so impersonal about business, and they do not care about what others think. They talk a lot about making fast decisions, but they do not seem to be concerned if their decisions are right or not. That is not very responsible, nor does it show consideration for the whole group. They have the same sort of inconsiderate attitude toward headquarters. They send faxes demanding swift action without knowing what kinds of obstacles headquarters has to overcome. Headquarters has a lot of requests from many customers around the world, and they need time to analyze them. The real problem is that there is no loyalty from our U.S. customers—they are very impatient and will easily leave one vendor for another, their decision based solely on price and turnaround time. Also, we are concerned that the salesforce has not worked hard enough to make our customers understand our commitment to them.

Step 2
Problem Clarification

Intentions versus Perceptions

Intentions	
Japanese	**American**
• Participate in the decision-making process without losing face • Stay in constant contact with the customer and Japanese management so as to provide good service • Maintain good relations with Tokyo headquarters	• Be active participants in meetings • Serve the needs of the customer and the company • Sell the product to meet personal and company goals

Perceptions	
Japanese	**American**
• The Americans are too concerned with action and not concerned enough about relationships with customers as well as with other Japanese managers • The Americans do not understand the systems at headquarters for the American market	• The Japanese are refusing to participate in my efforts to make a sale and denying the value of American customers • Headquarters is unwilling to make an effort to be competitive in the American marketplace

Japanese Perspective

The Japanese managers wanted to participate in the decision-making process, but they felt uncomfortable. "Americans are so quick to commit to a date or course of action without knowing the big picture," the customer support manager said.

> If something is important, or if we have something vital to add, it is better to discuss it one-on-one in a less formal setting, instead of the formal and rushed meeting environment. It is also extremely difficult to join in the discussion because everything is discussed in English at a very rapid pace. They need to slow down to allow us to think and respond.

The Japanese were hesitant about using memos but were eager to participate in face-to-face discussions.

> The Americans in this company need to know that it is more important to meet face-to-face than to communicate by e-mail, memo, or telephone. It is so dry, yet they expect us to adopt this style as if it were completely natural. In Japan, we rely on face-to-face communication where we can *nemawashi*, or share information and reach consensus. Americans use so many memos that we often say jokingly that Americans rely on "*memo*washi." I expect them to approach me and the other members of the executive staff personally to discuss important issues such as this. We should not wait until a large staff meeting for the first discussion; we should be discussing this well in advance of the meeting so that we know where each person stands and will not lose face during the meeting. The same thing goes for sending orders to headquarters—our people in Tokyo expect us in the United States to keep them constantly up-to-date

on the direction of the market and not communicate with them only when we have a rush order to fill.

From the Japanese perspective, the Americans were too concerned about action and not concerned enough about the needs of the Japanese at headquarters. Also, the Japanese in the U.S.-based subsidiary were not fully convinced that the American customer was worth the risk of pushing Tokyo too aggressively.

If we put a lot of pressure on Tokyo to fill this order and the customer goes elsewhere next year, we would lose much credibility in Japan and we, the Japanese managers, eventually have to go back there. The Americans should realize that we cannot possibly commit to any course of action or time line without discussing the topic in detail with the appropriate department heads in Japan. Besides, it is hard to know if the Americans really support each other, since they constantly change their minds during the brainstorming sessions. They need to put less emphasis on ending the meeting on time and more on meaningful discussion.

Finally, the Japanese felt the Americans had an inadequate understanding of the systems at headquarters.

Tokyo has many levels of management to consult with in order to determine pricing, specification changes, and delivery schedules. Too often, we send them a fax demanding an immediate response. The Americans assume one person at headquarters has information about inventory and production capacity right at his fingertips, but this is not the case. Many people are involved, so it takes time for them to find out the answers to our questions. Americans never take the time to approach us and listen to our side, they just keep pushing us to "fix the problem." The Americans have to realize that we are only a subsidiary, and that our older, more stable customers in Japan must take precedence over our new customers in the United States. Continuity and consistency are more important and reliable than making the quick sale.

American Perspective

The American sales manager explained,

I understand that the Japanese have some difficulty with English, so I always send out the agenda in advance. That is why I expect my coworkers to let me know, before or during the meeting, if they don't agree with my agenda or my objectives. I expect people to respond to the requests I send out. How can we ever get anything done if the Japanese continually ignore me and don't participate in the meetings? At all of the other companies where I have worked, it was common sense to send out memos to test the water, especially on critical issues. When people responded, you knew who supported you, who didn't, and what the concerns were. Therefore, once we convened a meeting, we were prepared to work things out.

She intended to serve the needs of the customer along with those of the company. "How can I sell effectively if Tokyo doesn't let me in on what is happening over there so I can relay that to the customer? I need to be a part of the information loop so I can be more effective in communicating the needs of both sides. As it stands now, I place an order and can only pray that they act on it."

From the American's perspective, the Japanese members of her subsidiary were refusing to participate in her efforts to make a sale.

> The Japanese managers contributed nothing during the brainstorming sessions. Their opinions and participation are valuable, so they need to learn to relax a little and join in the conversation in English. When they make that hissing sound by sucking air between their teeth, I know something is wrong but I don't know what. I wish they would tell us directly if they agree or disagree with what we are discussing instead of being so evasive. It doesn't help that they refuse to respond to my written requests in a timely manner. They need to let us know what they are thinking. I'm tired of the guessing games. Also, they were of no help when I was trying to get information from Tokyo. They seem more interested in not ruffling feathers than in building the business.

As for the Japanese in Tokyo, she had the same feelings.

> The Japanese need to know that the American customer doesn't hold the same loyalty to a vendor that the Japanese may be used to. Even long-term customers will abandon vendors if a competing company offers a better deal. If the Japanese want to succeed in the U.S., they need to compete vigorously in the areas of product price, quality, flexibility on specifications, and timeliness of delivery. Our customers expect a quick turnaround time on everything from price quotes to delivery schedules. I expect a direct answer as to whether they want to fill an order or not. I am tired of the evasive answers such as "We are studying it" or "That might be difficult."

Step 3
Cultural Exploration

Expectations and Assumptions

Japanese	American
• Building and maintaining relationships is more important than accomplishing tasks • It is not always possible to act quickly without losing face • Talking a lot is a sign of childishness or immaturity • There is an appropriate difference in status between the subsidiary and headquarters, and corporate priorities should reflect this difference • Written messages are an inadequate and incomplete form of communication • Large meetings are not the place to aggressively put forward one's own opinion • The *nemawashi* process is the best way to share personal opinions	• Accomplishing tasks builds face or credibility and is more important than building relationships during work hours • Objectives must be achieved within the specified time frame • Being open and talkative is a sign of honesty • Subsidiary customers are just as important as headquarters customers • Written communication is adequate for virtually any kind of exchange • Group meetings create synergy: "two heads are better than one" • Brainstorming saves time and results in higher creativity

Japanese Perspective

For the Japanese, the concern over losing face is much more pervasive. An American might lose face in the eyes of a customer for failing to make a delivery on time, but the Japanese would lose face in the eyes of everyone who is aware of the failure, including friends and coworkers. Americans feel guilt toward the person they failed when they lose face; Japanese feel shame in the eyes of their group, a serious matter for the Japanese. In Japanese culture, shame is damaging to both pride and image. Appropriate social behavior is considered to be the ultimate giver of grace. From a Japanese perspective, face is honor and integrity, the integrity of behaving appropriately (harmoniously) within a group. The Japanese feel that Americans do not seem to lose face because there seem to be no fixed norms of behavior in American groups. Another important thing for Americans to remember is that Japanese loss of face can occur between two friends as well as between an individual and a group. For the Japanese, the line between professional relationships and personal relationships is thin. Violating the norms of behavior in front of your coworkers is just as embarrassing as behaving inappropriately in front of your customers or friends.

Face is also an issue when it comes to the Japanese unwillingness to participate in American-style meetings, especially manifest in their concern about the face of others. If another person in a meeting makes a comment they disagree with, Japanese will usually not say they disagree for fear the other person will lose face. They will usually remain quiet, then attempt to discuss the matter in private on a one-to-one basis. If pushed to answer (usually by aggressive Americans), the Japanese often make a hissing sound by sucking air through their teeth and may add "That is difficult."

Americans tend to assume that decisions can be made quickly in a meeting through brainstorming, throwing all your ideas on the table regardless of their validity. Then you simply sort through them, weeding out the ones that don't work and focusing on those that seem potentially useful. This is an aspect of American pragmatism or instrumentalism in which ideas can be disconnected from the ego and seen as tools in problem solving. In this kind of brainstorming, withholding judgment is the norm, but the Japanese find it difficult to withhold judgment or to believe others are doing so. Thus, there is for the Japanese a high risk of losing face by making comments or judgments without having fully researched and considered the issue. Because Americans are not as concerned with face inside the boundaries of the organization, they feel free to speak their minds, knowing that they might have to retract or change their statements at some future date. For the Japanese, on the other hand, being forced to change a position or a decision after it has been shared in public would be a violation of their face within the company. It would be even worse if their decision was communicated to the customer or someone else outside the company and then changed at some later date. The unwillingness of the Japanese in this case to comment on the American proposal occurred not because they didn't have an opinion but because they had not been approached in a way they considered appropriate. If the sales manager had talked with each of her Japanese managers privately, preferably one-to-one, in the *nemawashi* style, she would have had a much better chance of getting their candid opinions. Since she relied upon the group meeting, which is the common sense approach in the States, the Japanese were not open with their feelings. Unfortunately, such hesitancy is often perceived by Americans as dishonesty or lack of openness. Either perception can result in distrust.

Unlike Americans, the Japanese rely on communication beyond the word, either written or spoken. The Japanese belief that each situation is different and must be treated within its own context, in combination with their desire to engage in personal relationships, leads them to interpret meaning from more than just words—that is, from nonverbal behavior and the situation or context itself. This, as noted earlier, makes for a high-context culture. As a result, they do not consider written messages (such as memoranda) as an adequate or efficient form of communication. Even when communicating with headquarters in Japan, the Japanese do not consider e-mail or faxes a replacement for regular conversations on the telephone. Indeed, it is considered an insult to send someone a memo or e-mail when you could easily walk down the hall and deliver the message in person. Also, there is less emphasis among Japanese on individual accountability than on the effectiveness of interpersonal communication. When solving a problem, finding individual blame is not as important to the Japanese as fixing the communication system so that informed decisions can be made. They see Americans as needing to assign blame, which demonstrates a lack of feeling for the face of the person who made the mistake and, hence, for whatever significance the relationship has.

Another Japanese value which comes into play is their acceptance of hierarchy between subsidiary and headquarters. The Japanese believe that a subsidiary is a second-class citizen in the corporate world, a child company (*kogaisha*) in a family of companies. The parents don't have enough money to make the child happy, so they expect the child to be patient and wait for the time when there are enough resources for everyone. But headquarters is not surprised when its young subsidiary demands more than can be provided or is impatient when responses are slow in coming. Such behavior is normal for a child. Headquarters also expects the subsidiary to understand its place in the corporate family. A subsidiary that insults headquarters too frequently can find itself disciplined like an unruly child. This attitude is in direct contradiction to the American value of equity, which we have discussed previously at some length.

American Perspective

In general Americans are very task-oriented—they place a higher priority on accomplishing tasks than on building relationships. In the case of the American sales manager in this chapter, task orientation meant getting the delivery to the customer on time, hence, the choice to conduct a brainstorming meeting. Brainstorming accomplishes many objectives at once; it fosters creativity, team building, and collaborative problem solving. It also saves time. This task orientation is a result of the historic ideals of capitalism in the United States. The dream of American capitalism is that through hard work anyone can become financially successful. Since the industrial revolution, Americans have been driven by the prospect of rewards for high productivity. In modern American corporations this translates into performance-appraisal systems which are results-driven. The American emphasis on getting results over building relationships has also come about as a result of the expectation that professional relationships are different from personal relationships. In a professional environment, people are expected to strive to overcome obstacles in order to be efficient. It is expected that they will put their personal problems and differences aside and will get the job done. This attitude, which may seem to some people from other cultures inhuman or unfeeling, is made possible by the knowledge that workers will have the opportunity to pursue personal relationships after work during their own time.

Americans are also concerned with achieving objectives within a given time frame, a value that is shared by the Japanese. The conflict in this chapter resulted not only from the differences between the American and Japanese cultures but also from the different roles that the Americans and the Japanese were playing in the organization. The Americans were playing the role of the salesperson taking an order, while the Japanese were playing the role of the manufacturer providing a product. The emphasis of the salesperson on timely delivery is common in both cultures, as is the emphasis of the manufacturer on leeway. It is also common in both countries to want to maintain good relationships with long-standing customers, but they differ in how they perceive customer loyalty. Traditionally, in the United States the free-market economy has encouraged customers to buy the best products at the best prices—regardless of who provided it. Customer loyalty is not derived from past performance; it must be earned every day. In Japan headquarters was acting from a broader perspective, meaning the potential loyalty of the new customer in the unstable American commercial environment against the loyalty of existing customers in an environment where loyalty and long-term relationships are more highly valued.

Another fundamental precept which comes into play here is the American belief that openness reflects honesty. The conflict was caused not because the Japanese do not value honesty (they do) but because Americans see openness as an essential component of honesty. If an American asks someone a question and that person doesn't reply right away, or if the person doesn't respond to the question or responds vaguely, then the American tends to question the honesty or at least the reliability of that person. Honesty means, from an American perspective, that people freely express exactly what they think whenever the occasion demands it.

Americans get upset when they think the customer groups in Japan get preferential treatment "just because they're Japanese." One manager confided,

> I would understand the Japanese giving a Japanese customer a higher allotment if their purchasing volume was higher, but to do it just because they have a long history of business leaves me defenseless. To make matters worse, I wish the Japanese at headquarters would level with me. If they have no intention of filling the orders of my U.S. customers, I would much prefer an honest reply. Instead, my Japanese counterparts are always saying "Let me think about it" or "This will be very difficult."

This belief comes, in part, from the American conviction that there is a relatively simple objective truth in every situation that can be expressed in words. Americans believe strongly in the communicative power of words (whether spoken or written, but especially written), which is why they believe that everything they need to know about a situation can be communicated through written memoranda. For Americans, the written word is accurate, it is efficient, and it provides a useful record of their actions. This is important because individuals are seen as accountable and therefore act to protect themselves from blame. Things such as spoken words or nonverbal communication are usually not recorded and are therefore of less value from the perspective of establishing whether someone acted responsibly or not.

The final American value at work in this situation was the emphasis on protecting one's face. The Japanese are often surprised to hear that Americans are concerned about losing face. This is because Americans do such things as change their minds in public and openly challenge each other, sometimes regardless of rank. In Japan, these behaviors would result in a loss of face. Loss of face or credibility in American culture is connected with failure to meet a commitment or an obligation or to do something you were supposed to do. The failure causes a loss of face as well as feelings of guilt. It should be kept in mind, though, that loss of face is an important dimension of the American psyche but not a paramount one.

Step 4
Organizational Exploration

Global Imperatives

Local Conditions

Japanese	American
• It is vital to deliver the product to long-standing domestic Japanese customers	• It is vital to deliver the product on time, with specifications according to the customer's wishes
• It is not necessary or desirable to let the American salesperson know about difficulties at headquarters	• Large sales orders will meet company goals and help the subsidiary become self-sufficient

Japanese Perspective (Global Imperatives)

The global imperatives influencing the actions of the Japanese were quite complicated. Shortly before the American sales manager faxed the order from her American customer, headquarters had received another large order from an established Japanese customer. They had already promised to deliver this large Japanese order, and they realized that fulfilling their promise would diminish their monthly supply below what they would need to fill the American order. The managers at headquarters were embarrassed by this state of affairs and were delaying their response in order to make sure their information was accurate. It is not uncommon for Japanese at headquarters to offer minimal "insider" information to the Americans at the subsidiary-level company.

The American's request for changes in the specifications was also a problem. The Japanese manufacturers were set up to provide their product for customers who didn't need changes in specifications, and their technical specialists predicted that a delay would be necessary to adapt to the American customer's requests. Filling the American order would therefore probably have meant delaying delivery of the product to the national account in Japan, even assuming they were able to find more product. From the Japanese perspective, the Americans should have asked if the technical change could be made (and waited for a response) before promising delivery to the customer.

Compounding these problems was the fact that the administrators at headquarters weren't convinced of the potential for future business with this new American customer. They were aware, indeed, of the tendency of American customers to "shop the competition." As a result, they were not willing to sacrifice a proven Japanese customer for an unknown American one. This is not to say that Japanese manufacturers will not take care of American customers. If the relationship is sound and both sides are willing to work together, Americans can expect high-quality products delivered on a reliable timetable.

American Perspective (Local Conditions)

The local conditions under which the American sales manager was operating, on the other hand, were fairly simple in this case. First, she was under a great deal of pressure to deliver the product on time and with the customer's requested specifications. This was less a function of cultural factors than it was of her role as a salesperson. Her desire to fulfill the needs and expectations of the customer was driven by her knowledge that American customers are loyal to price, availability, and quality—not to the particular supplier. There is a diversity of suppliers in most markets in the United States, and customers tend to believe in the capitalist notion of shopping the marketplace for the best deal they can find. In addition, she was driven to fulfill the needs of the customer by the knowledge that the financial compensation of the entire subsidiary was linked to her ability to perform. The Japanese president had explained to her that the workers' bonuses were contingent on sales results. She knew that the employees would be very upset if they had to suffer because of her inability to convince headquarters to supply the customer with the product. Finally, she was under pressure from headquarters itself to prove that the subsidiary could become self-sufficient. Her great desire to fill the largest order in the subsidiary's history was, in part, produced by the knowledge that she could help her company achieve its goal of profitability.

Step 5
Conflict Resolution

The primary generator of conflict in this case is a downward spiral of mistrust due to cultural differences, withholding of information due to lack of trust or wanting to maintain face, and then greater mistrust due to withholding of information. This cycle plays out all too frequently in the information-gathering and decision-making systems of U.S.-based Japanese subsidiaries. Information-gathering systems at headquarters are often either inadequate with regard to subsidiary requests or inaccessible to subsidiary representatives. Representatives at headquarters often display a lack of trust in the Americans at the subsidiary, which leads to negative perceptions of headquarters in the minds of the Americans. These negative perceptions lead the Americans to become impatient with headquarters' requests for more information and more time. If this cycle is not interrupted, the systems, which were designed to distribute information and expedite decision making, collapse into systems which breed greater and greater levels of mistrust, frustration, and inefficiency.

Once the American sales manager in this case had calmed down, the Japanese president approached her and suggested the need to examine the breakdown that had occurred in the system. He said that he wanted to understand how the systems in the subsidiary and at headquarters could work together more effectively and that he was interested in improving relations between the Japanese and American workers in the subsidiary. The American agreed that both of these goals were important. The president then asked her to assist him in obtaining a more objective analysis of the situation. He suggested that she request the human resources director to help the subsidiary look at the interface of cultures in its decision-making system. The sales manager readily agreed to this proposal and met with the human resources director to develop a joint plan of action. They decided the first step in this process was for the internal HRD staff to interview everyone who was involved in the decision-making system: the Americans at the subsidiary, the Japanese at the subsidiary, the relevant people at headquarters, and the customer. Included on the interview team was a Japanese expatriate working in the human resources division, who interviewed all Japanese employees.

Once the necessary information had been gathered, the staff recommended that they conduct a team-building workshop for the Japanese and American managers of the subsidiary who were involved in the conflict. In a nearby hotel, the American sales manager, the American vice president, and four other American managers met for two days with the Japanese liaison to headquarters, the head of finance, the head of customer support, and three other Japanese managers.

The structure and facilitation of this workshop were crucial. It was, for example, very important to the Japanese managers that Japanese and American managers be evenly represented. For their part, the Americans were concerned that the workshop be held outside of the subsidiary environment, free from interruption. Also, they hoped the model they developed for resolving this conflict could be used as the basis for future team-building and training programs. On the first day of the workshop, the human resources staff, working as facilitators, started out by sharing their understanding of the system breakdown. They explained that the objective of the workshop was to analyze how that breakdown had occurred and to construct a system by which the informed decision-making system for sales could operate in the future to avoid this sort of problem. They also explained that the solution to the conflict would involve redesigning systems, clarifying standards, and building communication skills for better teamwork.

Having established their objectives, the HRD staff shared the data they had gathered in their interviews. They encouraged all the participants to tell their side of the story and helped each person develop a positive explanation of his or her own cultural assumptions and expectations. By explaining their own perspectives and listening to those of others, the participants were able to attain a greater understanding of the cultural roots of the conflict. By the end of the first day, the workshop participants were able not only to understand the actions of their colleagues but also to recognize the positive intentions behind those actions. Each participant was able to go home with a feeling of accomplishment and optimism.

The second day the facilitators began by drawing large diagrams of the various systems which had been involved in the conflict. For each step in a system, there were spaces labeled "Japanese Standard" and "American Standard." The facilitators asked both groups to explain how they knew when each step in each system was completed. They wrote the answers in the appropriate spaces, creating a diagram which mapped out not only the system, but also the differing standards or precepts which the two sides were using as guidelines. Once the Japanese and the Americans were able to see that they were using different standards to navigate these systems, they began to discuss how they could resolve the differences.

As common standards were identified, the group began to re-create the decision-making system. They agreed, for example, to modify the ordering phase of the system by including a step for communicating with headquarters before confirming a customer's order (which conformed, they noted, with the values Americans place on honesty.) It was understood that the addition of this step would take more time but there were obvious advantages to the customer if the salespeople were certain of their ability to deliver before accepting an order. Once an order was taken, other new steps were agreed upon. The American sales manager agreed to meet with the Japanese managers ahead of time, before a general sales meeting, in one-on-one discussions, somewhat like *nemawashi*. It was agreed that the sales team would make a practice of having dinner together on evenings following important meetings in order to provide a less formal atmosphere for discussion. All agreed to participate in training sessions on how to communicate more effectively with members of the other group—including, for the Japanese, training in how to read and write memos in English.

Modifications were then proposed in the process of communicating orders to headquarters. They agreed that it made more sense for the Japanese liaison in the United States to assume that responsibility. They also committed themselves to closer teamwork, especially in relaying information to all members of the team and to developing creative alternatives in those cases where information or resources were not available.

By the end of the second day, the design of the new system was complete. The following day, the American sales manager and the Japanese liaison presented it to the president and won his wholehearted support.

Step 6
Impact Assessment

The off-site meeting provided the model for a new training program. The training program, custom-designed to focus on all of the communication events that occurred in the cycle from sales order to delivery, rapidly emerged as a critical part of the overall plan because the training focused both on intercultural communication between the Japanese and the Americans and on their communication with headquarters. The consequence of this customization was that the trainees were strongly motivated to learn new skills because of the clear connection between the skills they were acquiring and the potential increase in the team's productivity.

It also became quickly apparent that the biggest stumbling blocks in the plan were the lack of information from headquarters and the policy that placed priority on domestic Japanese accounts. What was needed when problems surfaced was intercession by the subsidiary president, including travel back to Japan to act as an advocate for the subsidiary. This would demonstrate to the customer that the whole subsidiary was fighting for its interests and also generate more respect for the president among his American employees. Japanese presidents of U.S.-based Japanese subsidiaries are often torn between explaining headquarters to the subsidiary and explaining the subsidiary to headquarters. Subsidiary presidents who push too hard for their workers or American customers are often considered to have "gone native" by headquarters. But the president understood that he had to play the subsidiary's advocate at headquarters in spite of this problem. He also saw clearly that in order to be an effective advocate, he would need to exchange information regularly with his American employees.

In Japan, the president met with the vice president of international business, explaining the needs of the subsidiary and arguing for a change in the practice that favored Japanese customers over American customers, suggesting a better balance when production was limited.

Luckily, the international vice president was responsive and even agreed to become an advocate for the subsidiary. Ultimately, the practice of assigning priority to Japanese customers was dropped in order to give the American subsidiary equal product access. All too often, however, headquarters is either slow or refuses outright to change its approach. In those cases any number of negative consequences are possible, up to and including loss of market share in the United States and loss of qualified sales staff. Upon his return to the United States, the president asked his salesforce to contact the head of purchasing at the company which had previously given up and gone to the competition and offer a new delivery schedule. This was done, and although the customer's needs had already been met by another company, he was impressed by the new delivery proposal and indicated that he would consider the subsidiary as a supplier for future needs.

The subsidiary experienced a number of benefits as a result of the steps it had taken. First, its new system and training resulted in a significant increase in and improvement of communication between the Japanese and the Americans in the company. Employees continually checked with each other to ensure that communication was adequate and understood. Meetings became much more even-paced, and the Japanese were better able to understand and participate in what was going on. In addition, the time the sales managers spent at dinner together allowed them to achieve better teamwork through improved personal relationships. Thus, in spite of the fact that the system had been modified to include additional steps, the time it took to complete a sales cycle actually decreased because of reduced controversy and misunderstanding.

The administration of the company also became more active in the sales process. The Japanese liaison began accompanying the American sales manager on customer visits, allowing him to get a better feeling for the needs of American customers. As a result, he was able to become a more effective advocate for American customers at headquarters. The ability of the Japanese liaison to convey information about the American marketplace more accurately persuaded his colleagues at headquarters to listen and respond to the needs of the subsidiary more effectively. Finally, the president's trip to headquarters increased the Americans' trust in their subsidiary's leadership. Their ability to pass this sense of trust on to the customers improved their competitiveness in the marketplace.

Step 7
Organizational Integration

The results of the conflict resolution were recorded in a number of interesting ways. First, the American vice president presented the subsidiary's new system to headquarters during his next trip to Japan. Understanding how the subsidiary was operating stimulated the headquarters staff to become more active participants in the American system. The success of the new American system also reflected well on the international vice president, who made sure the American's presentation was recorded for the benefit of other subsidiaries around the world.

At the American subsidiary, the human resources manager classified the new training courses as "core competencies" for managers. This meant that the courses were mandated for all employees at and above the entry-level supervisor, making them a permanent part of the training curriculum at the company. Each group of American new hires or transferees from Japan was required to participate in the training. The result of sales managers having learned these skills was that the Americans began to communicate more directly with headquarters. As they became better and better at this process, it was possible for the Japanese liaison to return to Tokyo and take a position at headquarters, which further facilitated communication because the Americans were dealing with someone they knew and who knew them.

There were no large, formal celebrations marking the success of the new system, but the employees at the subsidiary did find smaller ways to honor those who had taken part. The meetings and socializing of the sales team became regular occasions for them to reaffirm the value of their teamwork and their achievements. On a larger scale, the members of the company who completed the intercultural training programs were awarded certificates, which they were encouraged to hang in their offices. If a Japanese employee entered the office of an American employee (or vice versa) and saw the certificate displayed, he or she could feel confident of encountering cross-cultural receptiveness. The result was an environment in which the number of employees expressing a desire to improve their ability to communicate more effectively across cultures increased.

9

Job Skills

Case Study: Positive and Negative Feedback

In order for a company to be successful, its employees must possess the job skills necessary to perform well. *Job skills* are those distinctive capabilities that are required to accomplish a certain task, function, or role. This means that skills can involve thought as well as action, especially when it comes to solving problems and creating solutions to conflict situations. Knowing what to do is not enough. One must be able to adopt appropriate behaviors in order to accomplish tasks successfully. In joining a company, a new employee must begin to learn the skills for effective interpersonal and business communication in that particular workplace. Through daily experiences and some training programs, new employees learn how to communicate effectively in a business setting *with people from their own culture*. Americans, for example, learn to be direct and utilitarian in their business communications.

When Americans and Japanese work together, however, the culture-specific communication skills workers have already learned can be more of a hindrance than an asset in a multicultural environment. The communication skills that are most often necessary in U.S.-based Japanese subsidiaries (beyond those required for technical task performance) are those involving skills of interpersonal communication across cultures. These job skills enable the building of relationships and the sharing of information, which are necessary both for teamwork and job performance. Without such intercultural communication skills, however, the communication that occurs between Japanese and American coworkers is frequently inadequate to accomplish tasks, develop teamwork, and solve problems. When difficulties arise, avoidance and frustration or confrontation and anger can easily result.

In the context of this chapter, the particular job skill that is missing is the ability to give and receive positive and negative feedback. Even if the system for communicating information for appropriate decision making is in place (as in the previous chapter), and even if the standards that enable us to move from point to point in the system are known, the communication skills required to give and receive feedback along each step in the system may still be missing. The lack of such skills can produce a vicious cycle of misunderstanding, as each side increasingly shuts itself off from the other. A lack of communication creates suspicion and distrust, which creates an even greater unwillingness to communicate. At best, management is unable to convey its wants and needs, and workers are unable to adapt to the desires of their managers or express their concerns.

Step 1
Problem Identification

A. Statement of the Problem

The effective use of positive and negative feedback as a motivational or developmental tool across cultures is, at best, a difficult and challenging task. In Japanese companies in the United States, feedback has been one of the most frequently cited areas of frustration for Japanese managers and their American subordinates. If used effectively, critical feedback can be a powerful managerial tool for motivating employees to change or improve their work habits. If, on the other hand, feedback is used in a manner that is not acceptable to the recipient, it can cause serious morale problems. The process of giving positive and negative feedback is strongly influenced by culture, and the cultures of Japan and the United States vary substantially in defining the appropriate ways of doing so. Because these differences are not understood and because workers do not have the skills to manage or overcome their differences on their own, conflicts over feedback are all too common.

There are four major issues which tend to spark cultural conflict here:

1. amount and type of negative feedback

2. amount and type of positive feedback

3. timing

4. location

Negative feedback. There are often differences regarding the amount and type of negative feedback considered appropriate. Japanese managers are viewed by Americans as giving too much critical feedback. They are also criticized by Americans for being too vague; they offer few details about what went wrong or what they expect. Americans are viewed by Japanese as not giving enough critical feedback and as not expecting to receive it.

Positive feedback. Americans and Japanese tend to disagree about the amount and type of positive feedback considered appropriate. This, of course, is the converse of the first issue. The Japanese are viewed by Americans as not giving enough positive feedback, while Americans are viewed by Japanese as giving and expecting too much.

Timing. Differences over questions of timing often erupt into conflict. Americans want feedback immediately, as close as possible to the occasion which elicited the feedback, which means giving feedback during work hours. The Japanese are more apt to delay giving feedback until an "appropriate" time (which, from a Japanese perspective, would probably be at a later time in a more informal setting).

Location. There are major differences regarding the appropriate location for giving feedback. Americans are usually comfortable giving and receiving feedback in the workplace. Also, if the feedback is negative and directed toward one person, Americans expect to receive it in a private, one-to-one setting. Japanese, on the other hand, more often prefer to give both positive and negative feedback after regular work hours and, preferably, in an informal setting. Although it may seem to contradict what has just been stated, the Japanese are more prone than Americans to giving negative feedback to an individual in a public setting such as a meeting. This is considered just another form of coaching and is the "right" of the boss to mold his or her subordinates. It may cause a little loss of face, but it also benefits both the individual and the group.

Conversely, in Japan managers often feel it inappropriate to give positive feedback by recognizing or rewarding an individual worker in a public situation for fear that it might discourage the rest of the team or embarrass the individual being singled out for praise. Instead of offering words of praise, the Japanese manager will give more negative feedback and say something like "This job could be done better; go think about what you should do to improve." The aim is to stimulate self-directed effort at bettering one's performance. In fact Japanese subordinates may not be happy with the constant stream of critical feedback they get, but it does seem to motivate higher performance. In the bars and restaurants where Japanese managers gather regularly with their superiors, subordinates, and peers, "aftercare" is provided—easing the pain of criticism received earlier in the day, communicating acceptance, and giving suggestions for improvement. In the United States, this process breaks down for at least two reasons. First, Americans expect a portion of positive feedback to go hand in hand with criticism, something most Japanese do not have the skills to provide. Second, while the Japanese system of aftercare provides them with a way of wrapping the negative feedback in the cocoon of acceptance and Japanese-style camaraderie, Americans are left out. It is not a part of their culture to spend that much time in the evenings socializing with their colleagues. They are also generally not invited to go out by their Japanese managers, who have heard too much about the American desire to spend time with one's family. This is another case where superficial information about a culture can result in negative consequences. Americans will, in fact, socialize on weeknights. It is important, however, to give ample time in advance so they can schedule personal or family obligations accordingly.

B. Description of the Incident

A medium-sized Japanese manufacturing subsidiary transferred three different Japanese expatriates to the same plant manager position over the course of its history in the United States. The first Japanese to serve as plant manager had what he felt was an incomplete relationship with his American operations manager. The American always did good work, preparing extensive reports in short periods of time and continually striving to improve. The Japanese plant manager was mostly happy with the American's work, but, since the American never responded to his requests to socialize after hours, the manager did not have the opportunity to express his approval. Being limited to giving the American feedback in the office, he usually only commented on areas where improvement was needed. In spite of this limitation, the Japanese plant manager came to believe that his operations manager had a great deal of potential. In order to help the American fulfill that potential, the plant manager sent him to headquarters in Japan for six months on a developmental assignment. The American was somewhat hesitant about leaving his wife and family for such a long period of time, but he eventually agreed to go when the company agreed to allow him a home visit during the assignment. The Japanese made sure the American was prepared for his trip by enrolling him in a training course designed to teach Americans how to work with the Japanese.

When the American returned, he found that his former plant manager had been replaced by a new one from Japan—who was soon favorably impressed by his American subordinate. The American spent several nights every week socializing with his superior, and the American's wife offered to help the Japanese manager's family integrate into the community. Because they spent so much time together, the Japanese was able to give the American a great deal of useful feedback—both positive and negative—concerning his job performance. Each time he did, he observed that the American took steps to improve. Soon, the two men had developed a close working relationship, and the Japanese counted his operations manager as one of his closest American friends. As the years passed, however, the American and his Japanese superior saw less and less of each other socially. The American still occasionally accepted his boss's offers to socialize after hours, but their social time together was limited. Nonetheless, because they had developed such a close relationship in earlier years, the Japanese manager felt less dependent on the after-hours social setting for giving his operations manager feedback, which he now did in the office. They remained close working partners.

After five years, the Japanese plant manager was reassigned to Japan. In briefing his replacement, he described the excellent relationship he had with his American operations manager. He mentioned how the American had helped him and his family adjust to the United States and praised his subordinate for understanding and adapting to the Japanese custom of building good relationships and passing on critical feedback through informal socializing. Pleased with this information, the new plant manager immediately began to develop his relationship with the American. But to his surprise, the American didn't respond, turning down his frequent offers to go drinking after work. In addition, the American's wife did not seem interested in helping his family adjust. Without the time together out of the office, the Japanese found it difficult to pass on needed critical evaluation and feedback. Confused, he began to think he had done something wrong. He was also uncomfortably aware that the American was also unhappy about their lack of communication. A year after the new manager's arrival, the American submitted his letter of resignation. It read as follows:

To my supervisor:

I am writing you this letter to suggest some modifications in the attitudes of the Japanese in your company that would improve the working environment, the sharing of information, the giving and receiving of positive and negative feedback, and the building of better relationships. I trust that my comments will be taken as constructive and that you will realize I am writing them with the best of intentions. I am obviously not obliged to explain my departure, but I will feel that my service to your company is more complete by making these observations and offering these suggestions. I hope they will be useful to you in improving the quality of the workplace in your company.

When I first began working for this company, I realized that I was not receiving the sort of feedback from my first supervisor that I felt I needed in order to do my job well. I would work long hours overtime and come in on the weekends to finish a project for him, only to hear him tell me what was wrong with it. Other Americans in my department had the same experience and expressed their frustration to me.

Then my first manager decided to send me to headquarters for six months. I took this as an opportunity to prepare myself for ultimately becoming the U.S. plant manager. The orientation I received before leaving for Japan and the time I spent there taught me a great deal about working and communicating with Japanese people, especially the importance Japanese managers place on socializing with their subordinates. I learned that through after-hours socializing, the Japanese exchange valuable feedback. On the job, Japanese seem unable to do anything but criticize. After hours, however, they soften up, and the feedback becomes more specific and constructive. And just by inviting a subordinate out, the manager is expressing his appreciation, however indirect.

I decided when I returned to make an investment in my future at this company by engaging my second manager socially. My wife even agreed to help me, in spite of the fact that it meant less time with her and my children. In the process I learned many things about doing business with the Japanese. I came to understand that his criticism of my work was a way of motivating me. Sometimes, during those long evenings, he even offered some praise. In the end it was clear that he really did respect and value my work—but it took a huge sacrifice. I gave up the richness of a full family life to establish that relationship with my boss.

When I learned that he was returning to Japan and you were coming to take his place, I was faced with the necessity of going through the same long process again (while, I must say frankly, dealing with the disappointment of not being promoted to plant manager myself). After talking it over with my family, I decided that I could not make the sacrifice again. My children are older, and my wife is not ready to lose me for more years. I had hoped to make our contact in the office a substitute for after-hours drinking, but it didn't work. I only heard what a lousy job I was doing or how I needed to improve, though you never included specific examples of what I should do.

I believe that you are a good person and potentially a good manager, but I am simply unwilling to spend the amount of time it would take over the next several years to develop our relationship in the Japanese manner. In spite of my disappointment, I have many good feelings about my time in this company. I have had a great deal of personal success here, and I have fond memories of the manager with whom I worked so closely for five years. It is frustrating, however, to see so many other Americans struggling with the same problem. Most of them never had the opportunity to learn how to work with their Japanese managers and experience the benefits they can get from it.

I hope you will consider these suggestions a gesture of goodwill. My new job is with a company that is one of your best customers, and I hope I will have the opportunity to work with you in the future. Perhaps we can do better as professional acquaintances than as superior and subordinate in the same company.

The Japanese manager was disappointed but also surprised to hear that the American had been trying to build a relationship with him. "He was aloof and dry," the Japanese manager said.

I had heard that he was a good performer and had expected him to continue being one, but he never impressed me. It is strange to hear him say that he tried to get to know me. After all, he almost never accepted my invitations to go out after work. He always seemed to be in a rush to get out of my office. He would come in very briefly to deliver a report and then leave. The same was true when I criticized his work, and he never spent enough time with me for us to get to know each other. I had begun to worry that I had done something to offend him, but if I understand his letter, the problem was that he did not want to spend time away from his family.

Step 2
Problem Clarification

Intentions versus Perceptions

Intentions	
Japanese	**American**
• Allow time for feedback in the office environment for the American • Motivate workers and help them strive toward perfection • Develop an after-hours relationship with the American operations manager	• Use a history of achievement as the basis for a strong relationship with the plant manager • Use office discussions to make up for lack of time spent socializing • Maintain a healthy family life

Perceptions	
Japanese	**American**
• Americans are too defensive to receive feedback in the workplace • Americans are too sensitive about receiving negative feedback • Americans are too eager to go home early	• The Japanese plant manager is indifferent to my hard work • The plant manager gives too much negative feedback • The plant manager expects me to sacrifice my family life to the company

Japanese Perspective

The Japanese manager had intended to allow time in his office for conversations with the American.

> I was doing my best to motivate him, and I was open to taking time to talk to him, but I didn't know how to keep him in my office long enough. I just wish he had accepted my invitations to go out after work. After all, the American was quite formal around the office, and our normal interaction was limited to discussing production results. Also, Americans are too defensive when you give them feedback. They never apologize for their shortcomings, and they never offer any constructive suggestions for how they might improve their performance.

From his perspective, the Japanese manager did not understand the American's complaint about receiving too much negative feedback.

> My American staff needs to understand that, as professionals, it is their duty to continually improve. They shouldn't become discouraged when I criticize them. Every job assignment is an opportunity to increase one's skills, and it is my duty to make sure my subordinates have that opportunity. Pointing out the need for improvement should motivate them to strive toward perfection in their jobs. I shouldn't always have to point out specifically what they need to improve upon. They should be thoughtful and perceptive enough to understand what is needed, based on the nature of the job. Also, they should realize that when I give them an assignment, it is because I trust them to do it well. That is a form of positive feedback.

Although the American's explanation of his unwillingness to socialize made the Japanese manager feel better about his own role in the misunderstanding, he felt that the American's complaint was not justified.

> Americans need to recognize that the manager's workday doesn't begin at 8:00 A.M. and end at 5:00 P.M. Building trust among workers and developing strong relationships are vital to success. They need to realize that it is very unusual for the Japanese to give direct, positive feedback. It is easier to be frank with each other when we feel comfortable with our relationships and when we are in the more informal atmosphere of a restaurant or bar and everyone is relaxed. Then we can carefully choose the timing and the feedback we give.

American Perspective

The American operations manager intended to use his history of achievement at the company as the basis for a strong relationship with his new manager.

> I had a good track record with this company, and I expected my new manager to recognize it and accept my need for more family time. I deserve that much, particularly after all of my years of hard work at the company. Even so, we never really hit it off, and I had spent so much personal time and energy building a relationship with the last manager that I had nothing left to give. I needed more family time. Apparently my last manager never even briefed the new manager about me. I feel like I spent five years investing all my time and energy and didn't get a return on my investment. I feel like I've been betrayed.

The American also intended to make up for the lack of socializing by talking to his manager in the office.

> During the day, my new manager never gave me any reaction to my work unless I approached him

and requested it. Even then, I only got vague
criticisms. I spent plenty of time doing business in
the Japanese way, and my family paid the price.
I expected the new manager to give a little and
recognize there is an American way too.

From his perspective, it seemed as though the Japanese
manager was indifferent to his hard work. "It doesn't matter how
much extra effort I put into my job—he always finds something
to criticize. He expects me to work like a machine, constantly
churning out the product without any regard for the toll it is
taking on me or my family. He's very insensitive." After years
of socializing with his boss, the American had become frustrated with the necessity of spending so much time building
relationships. "These guys expect you to keep sacrificing your
personal life for the company. Why do they always need to
have a few drinks before they can ever give any useful advice?"

This is a good example of what happens in many multinational corporations. The local managers know what is expected of them by the expatriate managers from headquarters.
Over time, however, local managers often become frustrated
with and sometimes eventually refuse to adjust to the needs of
headquarters and revert to a style they are more comfortable
with.

The American also felt that the feedback he got was too
negative.

Negative feedback is fine, as long as it is balanced
with some recognition of things done well. I realize that I'm not perfect, but my manager should
take notice of my accomplishments as well as my
mistakes. I'd like him some time simply to say
thank you for my hard work, especially when I've
spent a lot of personal time and energy on a
project. When he doesn't, it's really discouraging.
Also, when he does have something negative to
say about my work, I wish he would give me some
examples of what specifically went wrong and

precisely what he expects. He usually just says "You should know better" or "You need to improve," which is very frustrating, since it leaves me in the dark about what's wrong and how to make it better. I'm not a mind reader!

Step 3
Cultural Exploration

Expectations and Assumptions

Japanese	American
• Negative feedback should be given freely and accepted without comment, while positive feedback should be subtle and infrequent	• Although negative feedback is appropriate and acceptable, it must be balanced by positive feedback, which demonstrates respect and recognizes achievement
• Negative feedback implies concern and advice, rather than disappointment and anger, and it can be a way of motivating employees to do better or to develop themselves	• All feedback should be specific and concrete. Too much negative feedback without positive feedback implies anger, disappointment, and (in some cases) excessive use of power
• After-hours socializing frees workers and managers from the status-conscious office environment and allows more opportunity for quality feedback	• Insistence on after-hours socializing violates workers' rights to private time during the evenings
• Confucian-driven hierarchical society promotes a parent-child relationship between manager and subordinate	• Egalitarian value promotes an adult-adult relationship between manager and subordinate

Japanese Perspective

The Japanese accept hierarchical differences; they assume people will behave in a manner befitting their position within the social and business structure. Therefore, it is natural for a manager to deal with a subordinate the way a parent deals with a child, giving negative feedback in a way that sounds like an adult addressing a small child: "You listen to me, I'm the boss and you have to obey." It is also assumed that the subordinate will receive such feedback with humility, without being defensive or asking for clarification. Positive feedback is offered sparingly, as the Japanese feel it can cause the recipient to become overconfident, complacent, or "soft." "Why do Americans need so much positive feedback," Japanese sometimes ask, "when they should already know how well they are doing?" When positive feedback is given, it is often implied or in a subtle form, the subordinate being given increased responsibility, for example, such as managing a special project. It might also come in the manager's sharing more information with the subordinate or inviting the subordinate to important meetings. The simple invitation to go out drinking after work is in itself another kind of positive feedback.

These kinds of feedback can be given without overt, verbal compliments such as "I value your input" or "you did a great job on the last project." Such comments are considered *oseiji* by the Japanese, compliments that are excessive or unnecessary. Japanese recognize new job responsibilities as a sign of trust from their superiors and value this ability to read between the lines. The saying "Hear one, yet understand ten" is widely used in Japan and illustrates this concept well. They pride themselves on being able to understand the meaning of events based on their context, as opposed to relying on a verbal explanation. When these values aren't exhibited or appear unappreciated by subordinates, Japanese managers become frustrated or confused.

The Japanese also value the constant pursuit of perfection (*kaizen*) and feel that negative reinforcement is more effective than positive reinforcement in motivating people to work harder. There is a widely held belief among Japanese that giving negative feedback "hardens" recipients, thus making them stronger and more able to handle difficult situations. It is also a way for the manager to show the subordinate that he is concerned for the subordinate's development. This sentiment is expressed in the Japanese saying, *Shigoto wa shikarareteiru uchi ga hana* ("As long as your boss is criticizing you, it is good because he cares about you."). This is not to say that all Japanese are motivated by negative feedback. As mentioned earlier in the book, younger Japanese employees are often viewed as a "different breed" by their Japanese managers. It is not uncommon to hear Japanese managers complain, "Our new employees in Japan who are in their twenties are very similar to the Americans I now manage; they need a lot of positive feedback and they don't like to go drinking in the evening."

If a manager finds it necessary to criticize the efforts of a worker in public—something normally reserved for a worker who has committed a series of transgressions—the criticism will usually conclude with a positive statement about the worker's intentions. After a public criticism, for example, a manager might finish by saying, "I know that everyone in the company is dedicated to hard work and customer service"—including the criticized worker. Public criticism is rare, however, because of the damage it does to the harmony of the work group.

The rigid hierarchical levels in a Japanese company also affect how, when, and where feedback is given. The status-conscious office environment in Japan makes "role maintenance" a priority, so managers tend to take on the role of critical parent more often. The after-hours socializing provides an environment in which role consciousness and status differences are diminished so that boss and subordinate can talk more openly and deal more directly with sensitive matters.

Japanese culture makes an especially strong distinction between public behavior (*tatemae*) and the true inner feelings and opinions of the individual (*honne*). *Tatemae* provides the framework for the smooth and harmonious functioning of Japanese society, but it is not intended to be an untruth (lie). Rather, it is an expression intended to preserve the harmony of the relationships. Thus, the expression of *tatemae* is a demonstration of one's integrity. It also offers a format for giving nonthreatening motivational feedback in the office environment. *Honne*, the expression of one's true personal feelings, is avoided by the Japanese in formal situations, which is precisely why Americans don't see that side of the Japanese, since most of their interactions are in a formal (business office) environment. Americans are much more ready to express their true feelings in public. In the systematic, somewhat ritualized, and (to Americans) rather curious after-hours socializing with one's professional colleagues, the Japanese create a forum for *honne*. The expression of honest feeling, positive and negative, would, in the workplace, be at best unsettling and at worst disruptive to good hierarchical relationships and to workplace harmony. While this process consumes a great deal of time and may appear inefficient to Americans, it should at least be understandable to the American pragmatic mind. It works for the Japanese. Eating and, especially, drinking together fosters the trust needed to create a supportive environment for giving and receiving both positive and negative feedback. Alcoholic beverages, regularly shared, are the lubricant of good relationships. The regularity is also important, which makes frequent trips to the bar all the more necessary.

American Perspective

The American dream is that anyone can be successful in life regardless of birth, social status, educational background, or intellectual gifts. What is important in fulfilling this dream is working hard, doing a good job, and achieving something worthwhile. Even if only a dream, it imposes the ideal of equality on the American workplace, where everyone's honest effort is recognized and respected. This respect, when expressed between managers and subordinates, often comes in the form of a simple "thank you" or "good job" after an assignment is completed. It is especially important to show appreciation when a professional works overtime without extra compensation. The belief in equality also enables workers to communicate very directly with their superiors when they are discussing work-related issues. Since everyone is assumed to be equal in the ability to assess reality, workers usually feel comfortable discussing or disputing such issues with whomever they please.

In the United States one's personal life is separate from one's business life. When an American sacrifices personal time in order to finish the job, recognition of the sacrifice is important. The question of giving positive feedback in American culture is complicated by the Americans' low-context tendency to depend on words—written or spoken—to communicate rather than relying on the sorts of nonverbal or inferred messages that the Japanese are more comfortable with. Hence, the good intention of a Japanese to provide positive feedback (in the form of higher trust) to a subordinate by assigning him or her more tasks will not normally be understood as a compliment by the American. Without the *words* of thanks, the American is likely to miss the point or feel taken for granted. Being taken for granted means, to many Americans, not being respected. Another factor in determining respect, from an American standpoint, is providing valued workers with compensation equal to the number and significance of their responsibilities. As a result, if Japanese supervisors give subordinates more responsibilities without increasing their compensation, American workers are likely to feel that they are being punished or exploited.

These issues deserve careful attention. American egalitarianism creates the expectation that one should be able to work in an atmosphere of mutual respect and concern for the feelings of others, regardless of one's position or status in the company hierarchy. How this respect is shown from manager to subordinate is the key to the successful use of feedback as a motivational tool. Americans expect to be given specific examples when their work is criticized. In fact, they are frequently described as needing extremely concrete performance objectives in order to get anything done (see chapter 7). They tend to be uncomfortable dealing with ideas that don't have a clear connection to their performance, and they are often impatient with subtleties in human relations. They value open, explicit communication and have a relatively low tolerance for ambiguity. In general, Americans do not like to be called upon to guess what is going on in another person's mind, especially when that person might be thinking things that are important to them. An old American adage is "Say what you mean and mean what you say."

Giving Americans general feedback like "Try harder next time—you should know better" does not motivate them to change their behavior or improve their performance. Instead, it emphasizes the sorts of hierarchical differences between manager and subordinate that Americans are inclined to resent. American managers do give orders to their subordinates, but in deference to American values they often couch the orders as requests or suggestions. American adults (and many children) do not appreciate being given orders that are bare and untempered. The American won't accept a critical manager who says, "It is not my job to explain. It is your job to figure out what I'm talking about." A failure to give specific examples of what a subordinate did wrong or how to improve can cause Americans to become angry and/or to challenge the criticism. Understanding this dynamic can be helpful to Japanese managers who observe Americans reacting emotionally to feedback; otherwise, they are likely to conclude that Americans are unable to accept criticism. In fact, Americans pride themselves on being candid, honest, and level with each other.

However, if they feel that their candidness is not being reciprocated, that information is being hidden, or that the criticism is arbitrary or is being given in an attempt to demonstrate the authority of the manager, they will react strongly, perceiving the person giving the feedback as dishonest, untrustworthy, or overly concerned with rank.

As for the timing and location of giving feedback, it is largely driven by the need for personal time (often referred to as "personal space") separate from professional or work time. While in extreme cases American "workaholics" make the same kind of commitment to work that the Japanese do, most do not and are not expected to do so. What drives Americans is the efficiency of their work habits rather than the length of their working hours or the need to build relationships. They are therefore reluctant to give personal time to accomplish business aims.

Step 4
Organizational Exploration

Global Imperatives	Local Conditions
Japanese	**American**
• It is important for top Japanese executives to develop good relationships with their American subordinates • Employees, especially managers, should work as long and as hard as required to get the job done on time • American workers must be instilled with the attitude of continuous effort toward improvement	• Managers should socialize with their subordinates and peers, not necessarily with their superiors • Workers should go home by around 6:00 P.M. and not be expected to spend a great deal of time socializing after hours • It is often necessary to socialize with Japanese managers in order to receive adequate feedback

Japanese Perspective (Global Imperatives)

In addition to the cultural influences, there were a number of organizational imperatives that influenced the actions of the Japanese plant manager in this case. First, as a person who had received a high-level assignment in the United States, he was expected to develop good relationships with his American subordinates. Japanese companies are very concerned with the ability of their expatriate managers to motivate the Americans who work for them. Japanese managers are often offered training courses on working with Americans before they leave for the States. Once in the foreign environment, however, even those who have received prior training tend to demonstrate patterns of behavior that are the norm in their corporation in Japan. In part, this is because most of their training in Japan is based only on information exchange or analysis of case studies. In order to be fully effective, the training should also include experiential or behavioral components to ensure effective use of the new information on the job. In addition, most new Japanese in the United States discover that their English language skills are not as good as they thought. In this case, the plant manager's unease in a new environment was increased by his language difficulties. And, of course, he had the added burden of the expectation in Japan that he would perform as well as his predecessor.

He was also under pressure from headquarters to instill the attitude of *kaizen* in his American workers. This expectation— that Americans can and should be instilled with the intense striving toward perfection that motivates the Japanese—is particularly common in Japanese manufacturing subsidiaries. In fact, the pursuit of perfection through the *kaizen* process is part of what drives the Japanese to work longer hours than Americans consider normal. Although younger Japanese in Japan are not as willing to work late into the evening as the older generations are, it is still widely practiced. Many Japanese supervisors and managers say that they don't expect to have any personal time in the evening Monday through

Friday. They "belong to the company" during the week and consider free evening time a luxury rather than a right. After orienting the company to the *kaizen* motivation, he was expected to install the whole range of other systems that the Japanese have traditionally associated with an ever-improving organization. Unfortunately, as is often the case, he was expected to accomplish these tasks without knowing the culturally appropriate way to motivate American workers. Because headquarters considered *kaizen* as common sense, Japanese executives expected the American workers to understand it with ease. Their strategy was not successful, as was evident by the negative reaction of the American operations manager to his third superior's constant requests for improvement. The American's frustration with his superior's continually pushing him toward *kaizen* was a major factor in his decision to leave the company. This strategy also resulted in an increase in turnover throughout the company. Ironically, the reduction of turnover was another organizational imperative that had been imposed on the plant manager by headquarters in Japan.

American Perspective

In addition to the other issues affecting the American operations manager's actions and reactions were socioeconomic forces in the U.S. marketplace. Several local conditions contributed to his decisions. Recall that the American had worked unusually hard to socialize regularly with his former plant manager. American managers are often expected to socialize equitably with their employees. Going out too frequently with the boss can easily be interpreted as an inappropriate attempt to improve one's career prospects, bootlicking to ingratiate oneself with one's superiors by means other than performance.

At the same time, the American knew that in order to be successful, he needed to find out what his boss was really thinking. Americans in Japanese subsidiaries are usually familiar with the concepts of *tatemae* and *honne*, at least to the extent that they believe their Japanese superiors are not always saying what they really think. The American in this case was, of course, quite familiar with this aspect of Japanese behavior. His failure to establish an effective relationship in the workplace—having given up the practice of after-hours socializing—led him to believe that his future at the subsidiary was dim.

This is another example of an intercultural dynamic altering the way a person would normally behave among those of his or her own culture. As an American, the operations manager valued an "open door" policy, the concept that a worker should have ready access to his superior. While he would normally not have hesitated to go into the plant manager's office and speak his mind, in this case he remained silent. The fact that the plant manager was Japanese caused him to keep his mouth shut. Even though he had had a close relationship with the man's predecessor, he, like many Americans, succumbed to the stereotypes of Japanese indirectness and conflict avoidance and ended up "walking on eggshells" around his Japanese superior, finally writing a letter of resignation rather than leveling with him, American style, in a face-to-face meeting.

In a sense, this American adopted a *tatemae* approach to his boss, although as an American he should have been more comfortable being direct. This is an illustration of how a little culture learning can actually hinder cross-cultural communication. There are times when direct discussions of cultural conflict between Japanese and Americans are the better course of action.

Step 5
Conflict Resolution

The first critical step in achieving harmony in this case was the American's letter of resignation. Intrigued by what the American had said, the Japanese plant manager began to observe the interactions between other Japanese and Americans in the plant. He noticed that all of his Japanese managers were staying late at night and spending time on the telephone with Tokyo. In contrast, their American subordinates were leaving around 6:00 P.M. In fact, the plant manager himself had encouraged the Americans to leave on time as a method of reducing overtime and cutting costs. The plant manager also noticed that the other Japanese managers' relationships with their subordinates were just as poor as his had been with the operations manager. Taken together with the information in the letter, the plant manager's observations led him to the conclusion that some changes were in order.

To start, he had to get more details on where the Japanese and the Americans were having difficulty. In particular, he was interested in determining the effectiveness of the feedback style his Japanese managers were using and how the Americans felt about it.

He turned for help to the manager of the human resources department, asking the manager to conduct a series of one-on-one interviews with each American who had a Japanese boss. The goal was to get an honest appraisal of how each felt about the feedback style of the Japanese. The interview was to include questions such as the following:

1. Does your manager give you effective feedback?

2. Does your manager give you more positive feedback or more negative feedback?

3. When your boss gives you either positive or negative feedback, is it specific and behavior-based?

4. Is the feedback timely? If not, when did you receive it and when did you expect it?

5. In what setting does your manager give you feedback, in the office or after work?

6. Is the feedback (positive or negative) given to you in private or in front of others?

7. What suggestions can you give to improve the manner in which your manager gives feedback?

8. How often do you socialize with your manager? Is this an appropriate amount? In what way would you like it changed?

The human resources manager interviewed over twenty Americans using this approach. After compiling the answers, he presented his findings to the plant manager. The information was not encouraging. Most of the Americans expressed significant levels of frustration. In general, they complained about the lack of positive feedback, the abundance of negative feedback, and the feeling that, since they didn't go drinking with their bosses, they had few opportunities to develop a closer acquaintanceship. Two examples of actual events were given to the plant manager to illustrate the types of problems found.

Example 1. One manager explained how he was given the assignment of preparing a marketing report. The report was for a very important meeting the manager was to attend. This report took two weeks to prepare. The subordinate wasn't given much lead time and, because of the complexity of the report, worked many hours of overtime during the week and on weekends to meet the deadline. When he turned the report in to his manager, the manager "merely grunted, without looking up from his desk." The day after his manager used the report at the meeting, he called the employee to his desk and said, "You need to be more careful compiling your data, it was difficult to explain. Use a different format next time. Try harder next time; you are a marketing specialist and should know better." The employee became extremely angry and frustrated with this feedback. "He never even thanked me for turning the report in on time. I worked my fingers to the bone in order to meet his schedule, and all he did was grunt and criticize me."

Example 2. Five different engineers related the following story. They had participated as a team in preparing and presenting a technical presentation for the annual quality control conference. They had spent a great deal of time after normal work hours compiling the information and had to consult with many different groups to obtain it. Their manager attended the conference and observed their presentation. After the conference the Japanese manager approached them and said, "You need to use a more scientific method of data gathering in order to have a better presentation; maybe next year you will do a better job." After this, he walked away.

Of course, not all of the Americans were so critical of the Japanese. In fact, many said that if the feedback were simply more *useful*—negative or not—they would be relatively satisfied with their situation. Many mentioned that they realized the Japanese were working hard in a foreign environment and appreciated their efforts. Unfortunately, the opportunities to communicate were limited, so the Americans didn't feel they were learning as much as they could from the Japanese. They considered that a lost opportunity.

Presented with this information, the Japanese manager realized that there were opportunities for both the Japanese and the Americans to learn from each other and develop a more unified team. Both sides needed to develop new skills to help bridge the gap.

Working with the human resources manager, he established the goal of having all the Japanese in the subsidiary trained in skills which would help develop better relationships with their American subordinates. He also decided to train key Americans to work more effectively with the Japanese in the subsidiary. He agreed with the HRD manager that the training should be tied to observable benefits to the company such as increased productivity, decreased turnover, and the American adoption of *kaizen* as a working philosophy.

It was agreed that the Japanese managers needed to be trained in giving positive feedback as well as constructive criticism on a more regular basis. After learning how to give more concrete, behavior-based feedback, the Japanese were asked to commit themselves to meeting more frequently with their subordinates. They were encouraged to schedule one-on-one meetings with their staff, thereby demonstrating an appreciation of the American need to conduct business during regular business hours. In addition, the Japanese were asked to take more initiative in inviting the Americans to join them in social conversation during coffee breaks.

As for the Americans, their training focused on helping them appreciate the Japanese need to conduct feedback sessions at more informal times and settings. They were encouraged to invite their Japanese bosses out to socialize in the evening and to be willing to accept invitations that could be arranged without detriment to their personal lives. Company-sponsored social events were scheduled to give them all the chance to get to know each other better. Both sides, in effect, were being asked to step outside their comfort zones in order to arrive at mutually acceptable solutions to what was recognized as quite a serious problem.

The training began in monocultural groups, which were soon turned into multicultural groups so that the trainees' ability to apply their new skills in simulated work situations could be tested. Participants were asked to conduct role plays on feedback situations which the trainers videotaped. This allowed all participants to compare differences and to check their own progress in acquiring new skills.

Another part of the training involved programming the Japanese and Americans to engage in social interaction together, which resulted in groups of them going to local restaurants for "bicultural meals." This strategy was not without challenges, however. First, the Americans wanted to be compensated for any extra expenses incurred by going to the more expensive restaurants preferred by the Japanese managers. As a result, the Japanese made an effort to accommodate the Americans by going to less expensive restaurants. Second, in a short time the two cultures were grouped separately, the Japanese talking to each other in Japanese and the Americans conversing in English. This problem was remedied by scheduling one-on-one lunch meetings instead. Initially, the Japanese had resisted the idea of holding formal company social events. They felt such events were a waste of company resources. After attending several of the gatherings, however, they realized that the Americans were happy in these structured settings and that the lunch meetings contributed to achieving the aims of the program.

Step 6
Impact Assessment

The training programs were particularly successful. By including both cultures, neither appeared to be singled out for the problem. Evaluation tools and achievement scores were built into the program and were published as "team" scores, which had a motivational impact as both sides worked hard to achieve the same level of competence.

The success of the training program yielded a number of important benefits for the subsidiary. First, it became apparent that considerably more communication was taking place between Japanese and Americans. With that increased communication, people were developing relationships conducive to the sharing of feedback, especially since some of the skills they had learned were specific to that goal. Workers and managers were more satisfied, they talked about solutions to problems together, productivity increased, and turnover decreased. Customers were happy in those situations where they were required to work across cultures because it was apparent that the people they were dealing with at the subsidiary had better communication skills. The fact that all this was occurring increased everyone's respect for the leadership of the plant manager. The training process also gave the plant manager the opportunity to identify future leaders of the company. By analyzing the training results, he could make sure that the company was led by those who were most effective in managing cross-cultural issues.

Step 7
Organizational Integration

The results of the training program were recorded so that proper procedures would be clear for those who would conduct the program in the future. The human resources manager entered the achievement scores of the participants in their files as performance-review data and integrated the training program as a whole into the general employees' training curriculum. The video-based training methodology was formally structured for use in future training programs and provided excellent baseline data for evaluation and research. An account of the training program and its results also appeared in the companywide newsletter. As the social gatherings became regular, the trainees began to use their time together to celebrate the achievements they had made in both training and productivity goals. He soon reached his goal of training all the Japanese in the U.S. subsidiary and before long was well on his way to his next goal of training all the American workers. In other branches of the company, plant managers who had read the article in the company newsletter also made commitments to the training program.

10

Professional Style

Case Study: Communication Style

Although different organizations may perform similar tasks, there is a professional style that is unique to each individual company. *Professional style* refers to the overall manner in which a person or a company performs its organizational functions. When referring to an individual, style deals with how a person behaves when performing work, managerial, and leadership tasks. In the case of organizations, style refers to the collective behavior of all personnel in operating the business. This is noted as a characteristic of the corporate culture. The importance of style in determining organizational culture is familiar to both Americans and Japanese. A common example of contrasting cultures in American organizations lies, for instance, in the differences between IBM and Microsoft. Before the IBM corporate culture was relaxed in the mid-1990s, it was known for its attention to tradition, as evidenced by the "uniform" of dark suits, white shirts, and neckties. This can be compared and contrasted to the flexible working conditions and casual clothing of companies like Microsoft. The Japanese might recognize a similar contrast between Sumitomo and Sony: Sumitomo being a much older, traditional company; Sony, a younger, more entrepreneurial company.

If managers are not concerned with developing and maintaining a consistent professional style, then the organization will often end up with no coherent style at all. In much the same way that it is necessary to train workers to ensure they have appropriate job skills, well-integrated companies find it necessary to provide training designed to produce common professional styles. After all, the style that comes naturally to managers in some corporate cultures is often directly opposite to that of managers in other corporations. When the differences between those two corporate cultures are compounded by the fact that one is American and one is Japanese, conflict can arise. Also, when American employees are hired by Japanese subsidiaries in the United States, they often come from many different companies which have different professional styles and corporate cultures.

We will discuss communication as an aspect of professional style in this chapter for two reasons: (1) the Japanese and English languages are dramatically different, and (2) the *way* Japanese and Americans communicate is dramatically different. Japanese and English are so different that translation from one to the other involves dealing steadily with deeper meanings and complex connotations. Because it is nearly impossible to convey the meaning of some Japanese words to an American (and vice versa), people in a bicultural situation may attempt to rely on communication *style* in order to get their messages across. Communication style is the way we communicate, which includes the speed at which we talk, body language, tone of voice, and other aspects of how we interact. Unfortunately, communication styles in the two cultures are just as different as the languages themselves. This has important implications for business, as communication is the essence of any employee, managerial, or leadership function. Organizations cannot operate without interpersonal communication, even when a computer is the mediator. Communication style is therefore a central factor of corporate life and must be relied upon to mediate cultural conflict. Workers and managers in U.S.-based Japanese subsidiaries are all too familiar with breakdowns involving conflicting communication styles. The illustration we will use in this chapter is but one of thousands of such incidents that occur every day across the United States. Although differences in the way Japanese and Americans motivate workers—a subject dealt with extensively in the previous chapter on feedback—is a causal factor in the conflict here, a much broader range of culturally determined behaviors came into play.

Step 1
Problem Identification

A. Statement of the Problem

A fundamental difference in communication styles between Japanese and Americans is at the core of much of the misunderstanding and frustration in U.S.-based Japanese subsidiaries. Unfortunately, when referring to communication breakdowns, employees of these companies often say, "If only I could speak English or Japanese better, I wouldn't have these problems." Enticing as such a prospect might sound, mastery of English or Japanese is not the almighty key to overcoming cultural differences. Of course, improving one's ability to speak the language of one's counterparts in the company can be very helpful, but language ability alone does not guarantee success when working across cultures. A key axiom to remember is this: "Linguistic fluency does not equal cultural literacy." Japanese and Americans working together in U.S.-based Japanese subsidiaries find that differences in the *way* they communicate in office settings contribute significantly to misunderstandings and conflicts in the operation of the company.

B. Description of the Incident

A Japanese subsidiary in the United States had just completed a banner year. All of the company's goals were met or surpassed, and the subsidiary had actually gained a larger share of the market. As a result, the annual sales conference was held at a well-known resort in Florida. The hundreds of salespeople who were invited to attend the conference were told—in spite of the initial objection of the Japanese management—that they could bring their spouses at the company's expense and that they would have time to enjoy the sights and attractions of Orlando during the conference. To kick off the conference, a formal dinner was held at the hotel. In addition to the American director of sales, the Japanese president of the subsidiary and his Japanese vice president for sales were also scheduled to speak to the assembled employees. The audience at the dinner consisted of the American salespeople and their spouses, along with a number of Japanese technical support personnel. The Americans were all very excited, looking forward to celebrating their accomplishments.

The Japanese president gave a brief welcome. He spoke very little English, but the audience nonetheless appreciated his remarks. The president said that he was happy to see the employees at the annual conference and that he looked forward to the next few days of planning for the new year. After some polite applause, the American director of sales got up and introduced the Japanese vice president of sales. The American had planned that he and the vice president would give motivational speeches to kick off the conference. At this point, the Japanese vice president stood up to speak. He was about fifty years old, and—although he had memorized his speech in English—gave the impression that he was reading slowly from a script. His posture was rigid, his face was stern, and his tone was accusatory. Pausing after every word, with longer silences at the end of phrases and sentences, the Japanese vice president deliberately and painstakingly made his way through the speech without once smiling or changing his tone. He nodded his head at the end of sentences and after particularly difficult words, as if relieved to be finished with them. He also sustained eye contact with certain individuals in the audience for long periods of time, impressing upon them the serious nature of his comments. Here is what he said:

> Thank you for your hard work this fiscal year. We have broken many records, *but*...we need to be careful to keep our fighting spirit! Our competition is working to defeat us this very minute and we must not let our guard down. You have done a good job...but do not allow yourselves to celebrate.... We have no time for that. You must prepare yourselves to work even harder this year. The company has invested...a lot of money in new manufacturing... facilities. These facilities are now producing...our product. It is your *duty* to sell these products as rapidly...as you can. *You must not fail!* I hope you do a better job in the new fiscal year.

The American audience sat in stunned silence during most of the vice president's speech. Near the end, they began whispering amongst themselves and shifting around uncomfortably. As soon as the Japanese vice president sat down, the American director of sales stood up again, physically backed away from the Japanese, and gave him a look of exasperation. He then turned to the audience and, with a little smile, said "Disregard everything he just said. We are here to celebrate your fantastic achievements this year, so give yourselves a hand." The audience applauded. The American then said, "Enjoy your dinner, everyone" and gave the signal to the hotel staff to begin serving dinner. As the waiters began circulating amongst the crowd, agitated discussion broke out among the Americans. The Japanese vice president turned to the Japanese president and began to talk quietly in Japanese, while the American director of sales sat silent, looking very uncomfortable. This event cast a pall over the rest of the sales conference. The tension between the American director of sales and the Japanese vice president was obvious, and most of the other Americans were irritable.

"I simply could not believe my ears," the American director of sales said.

> Here we were, sitting at dinner with our wives and our husbands, getting ready to celebrate the best year in the history of the subsidiary, and the vice president started talking about how we need to do better! The whole point of coming to Orlando in the first place was that we wanted to celebrate our accomplishments. It was unthinkable that the Japanese would stand up and tell us not to celebrate. Give me a break! I couldn't just sit there and watch him turn the whole conference sour, so I did what I could to salvage the situation. I was supposed to give a long presentation, but I had no choice but to throw out my remarks and do what I could to make people feel a little bit better about themselves. Even then, I don't think it worked. In spite of my attempt at damage control, the mood during the rest of the conference was ruined.

"I was successfully communicating to the Americans, and my words were motivating them," the Japanese vice president said.

> They were sitting quietly, listening to what I had to say—in fact, some of them started voicing their agreement near the end of my speech. Then, I was rudely and disrespectfully treated by my American subordinate, who told them to disregard what I had said. I felt directly contradicted by what he

did—it was total insubordination! I just do not understand his behavior. I am still shocked by it. I was so upset that I had to speak to the president about it. As soon as dinner began, I turned to him and asked him if he understood what the American had said. He told me what he had heard. I asked him how the American could have insulted me so. The president said that it was outrageous. I told the president that we must discipline the American for this behavior.

Step 2
Problem Clarification

Intentions versus Perceptions

Intentions	
Japanese	**American**
• Motivate the salesforce to achieve even more and show appreciation • Fulfill the role of vice president as a prominent company official	• Repair the damage to the spirit of the salesforce • Defend the accomplishments of the salesforce

Perceptions	
Japanese	**American**
• The American audience was receptive to my speech and was being motivated by it • The American director of sales was rude without cause	• The Japanese was attacking the salespeople for being failures • The Japanese was insensitive to the needs and expectations of the Americans

Japanese Perspective

In making his speech to the American audience, the Japanese vice president was, with good intentions, doing what he thought he needed to do to motivate them.

> I have studied English all my life, but I have found it to be a very difficult language. As a result, I worked hard to make sure I did not make mistakes during this speech. I even memorized the speech so that my problems with English would not interfere. I was coached by a friend who had helped me with the pronunciation of each word.
>
> I did everything that I know how to do in order to motivate people. I even did what the American director of sales told me to do—I specifically thanked the workers for their effort. In exchange for my work, the American insulted me and told them to ignore me. I do not know what his problem was. Everyone in the audience was listening very quietly—very attentive to what I was saying. I was playing my role as a vice president of sales to inspire the salesforce to continue in their best efforts. It should be obvious to everyone in the audience that we appreciate their efforts. After all, we are spending tens of thousands of dollars for this conference.

From the vice president's perspective, the American acted rudely without cause.

> His behavior was highly disrespectful. In addition to making me lose face in front of the entire sales force, he violated the approach we had agreed on by not giving his presentation. I know my English is not very good, so I was relying on him to explain my comments to the audience. He was supposed to go into detail about our competitor's new product line and the new production facilities at head-

quarters. Instead, he said two sentences and then ordered them to start serving dinner. I could not have said any more even if I had wanted to. This American director of sales has complained to me before, implying that I do not know how to motivate my own salesforce. This latest behavior on his part is clearly another attempt to increase his own status in the eyes of the salespeople at my expense. I have heard him say that I was too stern and that I looked at people too long. He does not understand that it is my job to show the workers that we expect them to do better. They need to feel challenged if they are going to be motivated to give more effort. This is a senior manager's role. The American says I do not know how to motivate the workers, but he knows nothing about the job of the vice president.

American Perspective

In telling the audience to disregard the vice president's speech, the American director of sales was trying to repair the damage he believed the vice president had done to the spirit of the sales conference.

I was trying to salvage the situation because the Japanese vice president was destroying the entire mood of the conference. It's my job to supervise and motivate the American salesforce, and I can't do that if they all feel like the company doesn't appreciate them. You can't just bring them all to Orlando under the assumption that you're going to congratulate them for their hard work and then—with their *spouses* sitting right there—attack them for being failures. This is not the first time that the vice president has done something like this. He's infamous for criticizing Americans when they do well, so I made sure to tell him before the conference that people would be expecting a celebration. I told him to thank the employees for their hard work. I just thought there was no way he would make the same mistake in such a big event as he had on previous occasions, particularly because we did so well this year. It looks like I was wrong. I ended up having to solve the problem he had created.

From the American's perspective, the vice president was acting in typically insensitive Japanese fashion.

It was clear that he wasn't on board with the spirit of the meeting, criticizing the salesforce for not working hard enough. He's a traditional Japanese who is unable to appreciate the hard work we actually do. All he can do is tell us to work harder. I was disgusted that he would take this opportunity to slap the American workers down one more time. Maybe what I did finally had an impression on him.

Then they spent most of the dinner talking to each other in Japanese! Of course, any time they ever have anything important to say, they say it in Japanese so I can't understand. Who knows, they may have been talking about how to force me out of the company—but I don't care. I was not about to stand by and let him blow off the best year this company has ever had. It's just not right.

Step 3
Cultural Exploration

Expectations and Assumptions

Japanese	American
• There is no need to recognize achievements with a formal, overt declaration of appreciation—workers are motivated by continual reminders that they must improve	• It is important to pause and celebrate achievements before going on to more work. By verbally recognizing the success of the past, we gain momentum to succeed in the future
• Leaders should have a distinctly different style from their employees	• Leaders should be in sync with the style of their employees
• A colleague will act to save your face in public situations	

Japanese Perspective

The need of Americans to pause and celebrate success is very confusing to the Japanese. They believe that it is obvious when the workers have done a good job and there is no need to recognize their achievements with a formal declaration. Their bonuses will reflect their success. Because of the relative homogeneity of the Japanese culture (in comparison to American diversity), the long-term relationships and implicit understanding common among Japanese workers, and the nightly socializing many Japanese engage in, it is difficult for them to understand why people need to be told they have done well when they should already know it. From the Japanese perspective, it is impractical to stop work merely to celebrate one's accomplishments (though things like company outings that build teamwork are acceptable). Change is so rapid these days that one must always keep an eye on the competitor. Some Japanese suggest that the American need to celebrate causes them to lose their competitive edge. In Japan, workers are motivated by the reminder that they cannot afford to pause in their efforts. They are happy when they meet their goals, but they are motivated by further challenges. Workers who are used to the idea that one must constantly work on improvement would not be motivated by the recognition of prior achievements. The concept that there is a momentum in success does not carry as much weight among Japanese management as it does among Americans. The Japanese focus on what is yet to be accomplished and are motivated by future challenges more than what they feel are hollow words of praise.

In contrast to the expectation shared by many Americans that leaders and workers should exhibit the same style, the Japanese expect that their leaders should have a distinctly different style. From the Japanese perspective, a good leader in top management should behave with sophistication and maturity, maintain a proper distance from the average workers, and be paternalistic. Ensuring good leadership means being sincere, serious, and caring. Leaders are expected to be responsible for motivating their workers and providing visionary direction for the company. All of these concepts relate to style. The Japanese leadership style, which the Americans did not appreciate, communicates to a Japanese audience a leader's maturity, sincerity, and responsibility (*sekinin*). A firm, serious demeanor demonstrates commitment of the whole self to the task at hand. Anything other than that would look immature, insincere, and irresponsibly unprepared to a Japanese audience. The Japanese vice president in this case was not about to violate his role by departing from his leadership style. This emphasis on style is a common characteristic among Japanese leaders who are very serious about their roles. Along with the role of leader comes a great deal of status, and the few Japanese who attain a high rank have worked their whole lives to enjoy its benefits. A violation of role is therefore not a simple matter for Japanese leaders—it risks the loss of face and a lifetime of effort. Conversely, Japanese leaders can also behave very casually in the proper setting. Americans are often confused by the Jekyll-and-Hyde-style difference between how their managers behave during office hours and how they behave when out drinking at night. Americans tend to celebrate and joke both during and after work hours. Japanese seem stern and cold to Americans during business hours but can then appear to be almost immature or unprofessional to Americans when drinking at the local bars (*akachochin*).

There is an important intercultural dynamic that took place between the American and his Japanese superior that reflects a departure from normal Japanese and American behavior. The Japanese vice president behaved in a different fashion than he normally would in a monocultural situation. Had he been giving a motivational speech in Japan, he would have worked hard to achieve consensus with his Japanese management colleagues regarding the content of his speech. He would have sought their advice and would have behaved in a way that would reflect well on his position of leadership. However, not having consulted carefully with his American sales director, he did not anticipate a negative reaction from his American audience because he knew his intentions were good and his instincts correct—and he *had* at the beginning of his presentation thanked the Americans for their effort. The Japanese presumed that the interdependence among colleagues would cause his director of sales to save his face if necessary. Instead, he did the opposite! A Japanese director of sales who understood American culture and listened to a demotivating speech from his Japanese vice president would never have acted the same way the American did. He might have tried to repair the damage, but he would also have tried to save his vice president's face.

American Perspective

American expectations, assumptions, and values regarding motivation and success were clearly involved in this conflict.

Americans need to pause when they have achieved something—to celebrate their achievement and to be praised before
they go on. Whereas Japanese workers acknowledge their
accomplishments in many different subtle ways every day,
Americans are more prone to larger celebrations at greater
intervals. At a meeting following a very successful period,
Americans expect reinforcement from their leaders about
their accomplishments. There are several reasons for this.
First, Americans are trained to be independent individuals.
They don't have the kind of strong identity with a community
that gives the Japanese continual reinforcement. Americans,
therefore, tend to be uncertain about their leaders' level of
satisfaction with their performance. As a result, they require
verbal praise more frequently than the Japanese. They need
someone who is in power to stand up and tell them how well
they have done. They don't assume another's approval—they
need to hear it. Second, without the kind of group attachments
the Japanese have, Americans tend to deal with problems at
work more by themselves. Compared to the Japanese, who
gather frequently with coworkers to socialize and discuss both
positive and negative aspects of workplace life, Americans
don't gather with coworkers and socialize as much on a regular
basis.

Americans also believe there is a certain momentum to
success. One hears the influence of this belief in many different situations. An athlete who has performed well in the past
is said to "know how to win"; a company that has had a great
deal of success urges potential workers to "sign on with a
proven winner"; and leaders in every sector of society call up
the memory of previous achievements in order to motivate
their followers. Celebrating past success is therefore considered to be a key part in motivating workers and creating future
success. Celebrating the positive results of a company's hard
work also reminds workers that they are part of a community.
The suggestion that prior achievements are not grounds for
confidence in the future would therefore be seen as an attempt

to break the spirit of the workers. Americans don't often have the confidence that they are an important part of a company community. Celebrating success is a key element in building what little sense of community Americans have in their business relationships. American leaders are expected both to identify future challenges and to express confidence in their workers' ability to meet those challenges.

Another American value that comes into play here is that leaders should be in sync with the style of their employees. This democratic notion extends beyond the basic idea that leaders should understand their followers to include the requirement that leaders *act* like their followers need them to act. Because Americans believe that they are fundamentally similar to their leaders in both character and status, they expect an attitude of empathy and familiarity from those in positions of authority. An American leader giving a motivational speech might be expected to include humor, enthusiasm, and other elements which indicate identification with the audience. In a speech like the one in this chapter where the audience had just completed a successful year, an American leader would make sure to review the data documenting the company's achievements before discussing prospects for the future. Like any normal worker in the company, an American leader would feel free to put down the competition and praise the company's effectiveness in the market. And throughout a speech, emphasis would be placed on the leader's personal affiliation with the audience. Although (as we explained in the chapter on performance management) Americans maintain a professional distance between themselves and their clients, they conform to an internal, egalitarian corporate style.

It is clear that the American also acted the way he did because the vice president was Japanese. It is also important to point out that what the American did was completely out of line. It would never be acceptable, from the American point of view, to insult an American vice president in public. Americans normally feel a certain degree of interdependence with their professional colleagues, although not to the same extent as do Japanese. Still, the belief that one ought to support one's coworkers, at least in public, is widely held. In this case, the American director of sales assumed an attitude of *inter*dependence with his American salesforce and *in*dependence from the Japanese management. The feeling of responsibility for the salespeople, which prompted him to insult the vice president, was a defense mechanism that kicked into gear in this intercultural situation. That the Japanese were strangers in his country led the American to take the attitude of "I have to do what's right for my people." The fact that he alienated the Japanese vice president was acceptable to him because he understood that the vice president was only a temporary part of the company. American workers in U.S.-based Japanese subsidiaries often regard themselves as the permanent members of the company and see the constantly changing Japanese management staff as transients who have to be trained to be effective in the American workplace.

Step 4
Organizational Exploration

Global Imperatives

Local Conditions

Japanese	American
• New manufacturing potential and competitive challenges made it vital to motivate the salespeople at the conference	• It is not appropriate to focus *entirely* on business or give negative feedback in social situations. Words of praise and caution are appropriate as long as there is a balance between good and bad news

Japanese Perspective (Global Imperatives)

For the Japanese vice president, there were very important corporate imperatives which affected his behavior—the pressure to motivate his salesforce for better results next year and to represent his company with dignity and responsibility. From headquarters' perspective, the sales conference was an important opportunity to accomplish these goals. The company's support of the full cost of the conference for both the employees and their spouses only added to the pressure on the vice president to do his best. In Japan, spouses would not be present at a dinner for salespeople in any event. Their presence created an unfamiliar situation for the Japanese vice president, who was unaware of the possible loss of face his salesforce might experience in front of their families.

American Perspective (Local Conditions)

In order to understand the actions of the American director of sales, it is necessary to examine the local conditions which affected his attitude and his actions. First, there was a strong mood of jubilation among the Americans who attended the sales conference. The American director of sales was very aware of the mood of his salesforce and joined in their expectation that the sales conference would be a time of celebration. The Americans felt that because the company was funding a trip to Orlando for them and their spouses, the sales conference represented a reward for their hard work. The fact that the company had announced that the most successful sales teams would be presented with plaques for their accomplishments only added to their feelings of anticipation. The Americans were under the impression that the company had sponsored the conference in recognition of all they had done in the previous year—not to make them feel as though they had not done enough.

Another important local condition for the American director of sales was the fact that the setting for the speeches was essentially social. The audience was made up not only of the salespeople themselves but also their spouses. Everyone was ready to enjoy a fine meal at the company's expense. For the Americans, these factors made the stern and seemingly accusatory nature of the Japanese vice president's speech particularly unacceptable. In American culture, it is usually considered inappropriate to "air one's dirty laundry" in a social setting. When the lines between business and private spheres must be blurred, it is the obligation of everyone to make sure that any business discussion remains as general and as complimentary as possible. When the vice president criticized the performance of the salesforce and—in spite of his good intentions—appeared to be scolding them for not performing well enough, he caused the Americans to lose face. This might seem strange to the Japanese, given that Americans are usually not much concerned about loss of face in front of coworkers. (The issue of face was discussed in detail in the chapter on decision making and information management.) The difference was that the audience included spouses who were expecting an enjoyable social event. The workers suddenly felt embarrassed at not having provided it—which is how face is lost in the United States.

The final local condition which had a strong influence on the American director of sales was intercultural in nature. Normally direct, Americans will often soften their feedback styles when dealing with their Japanese superiors. This "walking on eggshells" is the result of two widely held beliefs among many Americans. First, some believe that the Japanese are too sensitive to handle direct reactions or confrontations. Second, other Americans have experienced extreme outbursts from their Japanese superiors after giving them feedback because of using culturally inappropriate approaches. (The topic of front-loading Japanese superiors using *nemawashi* was discussed in detail in the chapter on performance management. Also, the practice of using third-party intermediaries to resolve conflict is addressed at the end of this chapter.) For whichever reason, the American had avoided giving the Japanese vice president straightforward feedback in the past. When the Japanese had behaved in a manner the American had perceived as inappropriate, the American had been very gentle and evasive instead of giving him the kind of direct, honest response he would have given to an American. But this strategy backfired; he became so exasperated that his pent-up frustration got out of control, and he insulted his superior in front of the entire salesforce. In a monocultural situation, the American would have been more direct with his superior all along, thus reducing the explosive potential of his frustration.

Step 5
Conflict Resolution

If Americans are to communicate effectively with the Japanese in their subsidiaries or at headquarters, they need to know more than just the corporate culture of the organization and the challenges it faces. They also need to know the proper communication style in order to behave appropriately in a Japanese cultural context—a style which reflects the nature of Japanese language and which demonstrates humility (team spirit), effort, respect, and a broad responsibility for results (teamwork). For their part, the Japanese need to know more than just English and the conditions of the local marketplace. They also need to know the proper communication style in order to behave appropriately in an American context. To resolve the conflicts that occur, each side needs to be willing to listen to and attempt to understand and appreciate the perceptions, values, and expectations of the other side. As has been apparent in each of the past seven chapters, achieving harmony is the most crucial step in successful conflict resolution.

After the sales convention was over, the American director, in a meeting with the Japanese vice president, suggested that his superior was unfamiliar with American theories of motivation and demanded that he receive coaching in how to communicate in an appropriate style at such important functions. The Japanese was clearly very upset. He considered the American disruptive, argumentative, disrespectful, and immature and was offended that the American would question his ability to motivate his own workers. On the contrary, he suggested that it was the American who did not understand motivational techniques. After a few more meetings involving similar accusations and demands, the American director of sales decided to offer his resignation. He left the company shortly thereafter, and as time went by, the turnover rate among the American workers in the subsidiary increased significantly. Their relationships with Japanese management in general deteriorated. The Japanese president finally realized that he had a very serious problem on his hands.

To the Reader

In this book we have presented a wide range of conflict situations, most the result of some kind of difference in organizational and/or cultural characteristics between the Japanese and Americans. In each case, the conflict was worked through to a successful resolution via some form of cultural mediation. However, a group of skilled cultural mediators may not always be on hand to solve future conflicts. Simply following or trying to imitate the conflict resolution processes described here is not always going to be satisfactory. Each problem will vary too much and have too many unique aspects. What is important, therefore, is not the specifics of how we worked with a particular company but the general principles involved and the application of the problem-solving design and conflict resolution strategies. What we intend to do here is challenge you to work out a solution to this problem on your own. How would you solve it if doing so were your responsibility? We will conclude this chapter with a few additional insights into the most common conflict resolution tactics employed by Americans and Japanese and suggest you reread chapter 2 for further guidance. Our comments are based on our own extensive experience as consultants and cultural mediators and on interviews with Japanese and American managers and psychologists living in both countries. They are intended to help inform your thinking about cultural differences in dealing with conflict, not to be interpreted as stereotypic images of Japanese and Americans. All interpretations discussed herein have been products of our interviews with Japanese and American employees in Japanese organizations in the United States.

Conflict Resolution Style: Direct Confrontation versus Third-Party Intermediary Which to Use?

Japanese Perspective

The Japanese place a great deal of emphasis on creating harmony in order to prevent conflicts from arising in the first place. *Wa*, or harmony, is one of the oldest and most important Japanese values. In the workplace, a manager's job is to create harmony so that conflicts do not occur. When they do, the Japanese prefer to avoid direct confrontation. In their view, confrontation is more likely to cause the people involved to lose ground (and face) than to make progress. Instead, the Japanese prefer to utilize a third-party negotiator or intermediary (*chukaisha*), talk to each other at a later time under different circumstances and with a different atmosphere (*funikizukuri*), or postpone a discussion until emotions have subsided. In order to avoid confrontation, Japanese may even agree to something and then fail to follow through rather than risk open disagreement. If necessary, they may use an intermediary. Whatever the procedure, the Japanese believe one should control one's emotions in conflicts because of the risk of permanent damage to relationships. Things that are said during emotional outbursts are not likely to be forgiven (unless they happen after one has had several drinks and is speaking informally), and comments on someone's behavior are difficult to separate from comments on his or her personality. As illustrated below, if person A has the need to clear up a problem with person C, it is often the case that A will discuss this directly with person B to get advice. In addition, B may be used as a messenger delivering information to and from C.

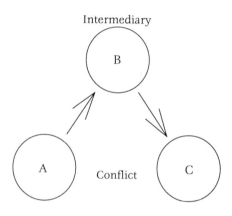

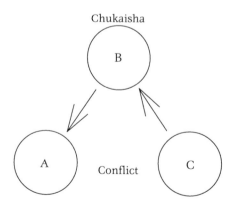

All this gives Americans the impression that Japanese are thin-skinned, while Japanese are likely to see Americans as the opposite—thick-skinned. Because Americans are always asking for feedback, Japanese managers assume they are not hurt by personal criticism.

For the Japanese, one key to resolving a conflict is patience, *nintairyoku*. When someone reacts to a conflict with pride or emotion, it is necessary to have patience with the person. The Japanese will try to create a good atmosphere that will defuse the situation and enable them to express empathy with the other party's feelings. Having bridged the conflict and created harmony, one party may then try to persuade the other to compromise or defer to his or her opinion. Ideally, these efforts at persuasion, which depend on reason cushioned by the emotion of the personal interaction, continue until one or the other or both sides yield to reach a consensus but not necessarily an agreement on the issues at hand. If an understanding cannot be reached, both parties draw back and postpone dealing with the conflict (*atomawashi*). As a result, nonresponsiveness on the part of Japanese may indicate any number of things, from discomfort and disagreement to a reserving of judgment or the feeling that the point that has just been made is obvious. Silence may mean that they need time to think or that they are simply comfortable with their situation. It does not necessarily mean consent—or disagreement. Some conflicts are even seen as best left undiscussed. With time, it is believed that feelings will dissipate or that the parties will come to a tacit agreement on how to behave peacefully in public together. If one side does make a major concession, it is considered to be the obligation of the other to respond in kind some day. One Japanese conflict resolution technique, *makete mi o toru* (stooping to conquer), involves the demonstration of so much humility and deference that the other party cannot avoid responding with a conciliatory gesture without seeming crude.

Given this information, along with the other insights you have gained from the previous chapters, how could you solve the conflict in this chapter? Make sure to approach the conflict from both roles. What would you do if you were the top American in this organization? What if you were the Japanese president of the subsidiary? There are many different paths to harmony in this case, and we are confident that some of those mentioned in the previous chapters or discussed in this one will be effective.

American Perspective

For many Americans, direct confrontation in conflict situations is a commendable course of action. It is common for Americans to deal with conflict without ever using an intermediary. As illustrated on the next page, if person A has the need to clear up a problem with person C, it is completely acceptable for A to discuss this directly with C. In fact, the ability to be direct is valued in American culture. One merely has to look in the "Interpersonal Skills" section of any bookstore and count the number of books devoted to the topic of assertive behavior to be reminded of this fact. In the figure below, the role played by person B may be as an adviser to either persons A or C, but it is not necessary for person B to ever become directly involved as a negotiator. This is consistent with the American belief that the most effective way to resolve a conflict is to confront the issues quickly, rationally, and directly, all of which reflects their lesser concern, compared to the Japanese, with long-term professional relationships and the loss of face. They believe that things said between two people in a confrontation should not necessarily affect their relationship. In other words, the conflict resolution process is often considered to be a separate world in which people may say what they feel without a sense of responsibility for hurting another person's feelings. In fact, Americans sometimes accept emotional outbursts as a normal part of the conflict resolution process. This phenomenon of letting off steam allows Americans to vent their frustrations without serious consequences. Even more common than verbal outbursts are nonverbal emotional reactions, such as extreme facial expressions or fists pounded on tabletops. By showing their emotions through their facial expressions, Americans demonstrate their conviction about issues and their trust in the person they are dealing with. From their perspective, hiding such reactions would be a sign of mistrust or a lack of conviction.

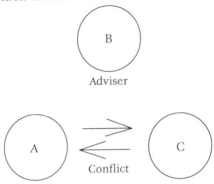

Americans also believe that conflicts should be discussed verbally in order to reach a healthy resolution. If no verbal agreement is reached, Americans will not feel that the issue has been satisfactorily resolved. Once this has been accomplished, however, Americans have confidence in the path to resolution. Speech is therefore an important part of conflict resolution for Americans. Silence during the process can signal that somone is closed to discussion or at least extremely uncomfortable. Nonresponsiveness communicates an unwillingness to cooperate or a lack of interest. It is expected that the participants in resolving a conflict will respond verbally to each point made by the other side. A classic legal saying in America is that "He who remains silent is presumed to have agreed." Americans normally want to make sure that their intentions are not miscommunicated. This applies especially when accusations are made by the other party. Americans believe it is appropriate to defend themselves if they feel they have been unjustly accused and often will not be satisfied with the resolution of a conflict until they have been allowed to address each of the other side's accusations verbally. Americans feel that the fairest determinants of conflict resolution are facts, logic, and truth. There is also a strong inclination toward compromise after emotions have been expressed and soothed and rational discussion returns. In fact, the desire to compromise will frequently bring about resolution before efforts to persuade by facts or logic have had an effect.

11

Conclusion

We began this book by pointing out the challenges—the dangers and the opportunities—inherent in the convergence of cultures in U.S.-based Japanese subsidiaries. While the eight case studies presented in the body of the book have certainly identified the dangers of cultural conflict, we hope they have also provided some insight into the opportunity offered in this kind of intercultural environment to create through carefully managed conflict resolution and cultural mediation a vital and effective multicultural workplace. Simply put, we have attempted to suggest ways to build bridges between Japanese and Americans who work together to the end of establishing productive and harmonious working relationships. In fact, the effective resolution of the cases presented in this book actually enabled the companies involved to deal more successfully with subsequent cross-cultural conflicts.

The areas described and analyzed are not the only ones over which Japanese and Americans clash. Our research and consulting over the last twenty-five years have revealed dozens of different kinds of specific conflicts that have occurred again and again in any number of Japanese subsidiaries. In choosing the conflicts presented here, we have attempted to select issues representative of those that occur most frequently in each of the basic domains that characterize business organizations and which were identified in chapter 2.

Corporate Values
Business Strategies
Corporate Structure
Staffing Policies
Performance Standards
Operational Systems
Job Skills
Professional Style

In our analyses of these issues, two dimensions of major significance emerge. One is the central importance of the balance of headquarters (global) and subsidiary (local) relationships in the globalization of world businesses. The other is the crucial role of the cultural mediator in managing those relationships.

Balancing Global and Local Requirements

We are moving into a new century in which business development is going to alter radically, not only becoming increasingly global but also finding a new balance between the developed and the less developed nations.

In the past, the richer nations entered foreign markets and foreign countries and dictated both the technical *and* the cultural terms of the relationship. This practice is no longer acceptable, and its rejection as an approach can be particularly noted in Asia among the former "four little dragons": Korea, Taiwan, Singapore, and (prior, at least, to the transfer to

Chinese sovereignty) Hong Kong. And, of course, China today is the primary example. They will no longer yield the kind of absolute control over foreign operations in their countries as was the standard in the past.

These changes are evident in many areas of international business operations. They are at the heart of the kinds of global/local issues that, as we have seen in the pages of this book, play such a critical role in determining success or failure in establishing a business in another culture. There is no escape or retreat from these sweeping changes. Trends in international economic globalization will see increasing numbers of companies wanting to establish large-scale manufacturing and distribution operations in foreign countries. In the process these companies will have to rely more and more heavily on local personnel, who will in turn increasingly question headquarters' strategies and operational standards and demand more engagement in the decision-making process.

In the intersection between local imperatives and directives from headquarters is the issue of control. To what degree and in what areas is headquarters ready to pass control on to the subsidiary and local managers? To what degree are local managers willing to function in the shadow of directives from headquarters? Every year, these questions become more and more important.

A useful distinction here is between an *international* business and a *global* business. The former is a company that operates within the framework of its home culture and simply transplants these operations to other countries while maintaining strong control at headquarters. The global organization, on the other hand, establishes operations in other countries that take on a new form, responds to the sociocultural environment in which it operates, and delegates a higher degree of autonomy to the subsidiary. Indeed, it may even modify its own domestic operations from benchmarks it learned from its subsidiaries, as IBM learned customer relations from Japan.

The traditional international model of strong central control with little regard to local conditions and culture is, with increasing frequency, proving itself a disaster. This is particularly true in the case of the Japanese and American interface.

Among the world's industrial nations, Japan has established a pattern of resisting foreign pressure to adapt to local needs and exercising strong control over the operations of its foreign subsidiaries. Yet, as economic conditions in Japan change, even the Japanese are beginning to recognize the need to mitigate the resulting conflict and reduce the breadth of control exercised.

This shift involves greater attention to the following:

1. integrating the organizational characteristics of headquarters with those of the subsidiaries, as has been brought to light in chapters 3-10 in this book;

2. clarifying the differences in expectations, assumptions, values, and cultural norms between headquarters and the overseas subsidiary;

3. dealing with differences not only on a case-by-case basis but also in the broader, more comprehensive context of both headquarters and local requirements. This effort will ensure consistency from one subsidiary to another and allow them to learn from each other and benefit from the inevitable synergy that results, instead of operating in the isolated "silos" that so often characterize Japanese subsidiaries.

The need for overseas subsidiaries to become more independent is born out of economic necessity. In the case of Japanese companies in the United States, domestic growth opportunities within Japan are limited, so the large Japanese multinational corporations can no longer subsidize their overseas operations. The subsidiaries must become self-sufficient, and in most cases this means distancing themselves from the bureaucratic red tape of headquarters. This process has resulted in a new breed of manager being sent from Japan to the

United States, one who is independent enough to recognize and deal with the demands of local operations, yet savvy enough to maintain good relations with headquarters. This is no simple task, since these managers are often caught between opposing forces: local customers, for example, demanding faster decisions or quicker delivery of goods and headquarters giving priority to domestic customers and reacting slowly to overseas imperatives.

Clearly there has been an evolution in the way the Japanese are attempting to manage the cultural differences that plague their efforts to manage their subsidiaries in the United States. Indeed, in recent years "Americanization" of the subsidiaries has become a fad, though in policy only. This stated intention to Americanize may bring about some reduction in conflict, but it requires a practical management style that not only suits the particulars of the American setting but that deals with all the treacherous cultural crosscurrents to which modern global business organizations are subject.

Achieving Synergy and the Role of the Cultural Mediator

If global/local issues lie at the heart of the conflict in multinational companies, the cultural mediator lies at the heart of the solution.

In attempting to deal with the conflict which is the subject of this book, it is not enough to focus narrowly on the process of conflict resolution. What the headquarters and subsidiaries must do is collaborate in the broadest sense on the development of a synergistic organizational culture. Quite simply, this means developing a unique "third culture" in which the perspectives of both cultures are integrated at various levels throughout the organization.

In the case of Japanese subsidiaries in the United States, the development of a third culture, in which the needs of both

Japanese and Americans are taken into account, results in an organization dramatically different from and functionally more effective than the two separate cultures operating in tandem while vying for control of every decision. This is a big order and calls for a great deal of learning and commitment to seeking consensus or making compromises regarding deeply held beliefs and ingrained behaviors. Most important: trusting in luck is the least efficient way to achieve synergy. Though many people refuse to recognize it, unmanaged or ineffectively managed cross-cultural conflict is very debilitating, if not destructive, in most organizations. Synergy emerges from the conscious process of resolving conflict and integrating different personal and operational perspectives, and it requires leadership or at least intercession in the form of a trained, skilled mediator.

While the word *culture* is bandied about rather freely in the corporate world today—particularly within the framework of "corporate culture"—its critical importance in bicultural or multicultural organizations is seldom fully understood. It is in the confrontation of just these deeply held cultural beliefs and ingrained behaviors that the root of the problem may be found. Lurking behind the beliefs we have about business strategy, business structures, business systems, and business standards are more fundamental cultural assumptions and values based on the way we have been taught by our culture to view the world. These perspectives are usually different from the values and assumptions of people from other cultures, which become most evident and obstructive when we attempt to integrate role functions in a dynamic business organization.

The conflicts resulting from these differences are not easily resolved. They are certainly not solved for Americans by learning how to offer a business card to Japanese, or even by mastering the Japanese language, as valuable as that may be. They are solved by addressing the fundamental differences in values and behaviors, in intentions and perceptions, in expectations and assumptions, and in corporate and local imperatives. This calls not only for understanding the role cultural differences play but also for dealing with them through a skilled mediation process.

The mediator role has special challenges. Even when those who are directly involved in a cross-cultural conflict have attempted to take into account every possible reason for the incident or misunderstanding, there are still problems to overcome. Those in conflict may not be fully aware of how much their own cultural assumptions and expectations (their own common sense) may be influencing them. They may not take into account all the cultural factors at work in the organizational environment. The antidote is a skilled third-party intervention, which may come either from a trained staff member or from someone outside the organization. The ability to serve as a cultural mediator requires a specific set of competencies:

- a degree of bilingual capability
- disciplined and systematic understanding of the sources of the values and mindsets that tend to be dominant in each culture
- appreciation of and sensitivity to the distinct variations of values and behaviors in each culture
- interactive listening skills and the patience to explore hidden meanings
- the ability to empathize with and understand others, and to respect alternative interpretations of what is happening or has happened
- the ability to comprehend the differences of meaning that result from the discovery that one person's intention is not necessarily accurately interpreted by another
- a high tolerance for ambiguity and uncertainty along with the willingness to persevere in the commitment to achieve harmony
- tolerance for role flexibility (Cultural mediators cannot

presume that their role will always be the same. The mediator may need to be a problem solver, a facilitator, a mediator, or an educator; or he or she may take on any of a number of other roles, depending on the client, context, location, and corporate culture.)

- the ability to trust that the solution lies within those in conflict as much as within one's own ability to facilitate resolution

Cultural mediation also requires that the cultural mediator must (1) be present throughout the conflict resolution process, (2) be or become thoroughly conversant with the global and local pressures in the organization and where they face off most strongly, and (3) be joined by a comediator from the other culture. No matter how skilled your principal mediator is, there are still going to be dimensions of the conflict to which he or she will be culturally blind. Also, participants will inevitably attribute to the mediator bias against their culture, ethnicity, or race. The comediator must have the objectivity, linguistic skills, and empathetic capability of the principal mediator but does not need to be as highly trained.

The cultural mediator plays a critical role, but one that particularly high-powered executives frequently have difficulty accepting. They often perceive culture as "soft" and not entirely real, and cultural problems as ones that any intelligent person can solve. But when a company has difficulties with its multisystemmed computer operations, an executive with an MBA doesn't generally try to fix them him- or herself. A computer engineer is given the job. So should a cultural mediator be given the job of dealing with cross-cultural difficulties.

All important is the commitment that must be made to the development of a synergistic organizational culture that is acceptable to both sides and, indeed, builds the "third culture" mentioned earlier. If we look at conflict from only one angle, we can resolve only one part of the problem—and more likely none of it. In each of the eight cases we have presented in this book, a key component in the conflict resolution was the ability of those involved to eventually see the issue from the other person's point of view. It is the function of the cultural mediator both to achieve that kind of empathy and to help the participants in the dispute achieve it as well.

It should be noted that this does not mean that companies never resolve culture-based conflicts in other ways. Indeed, a number of Japanese subsidiaries, especially in the auto industry, for example, have worked their way through unmanaged cross-cultural confrontations and have emerged with viable operational structures and advantageous trade-offs. For instance, the Americans ultimately accept just-in-time inventory and certain highly functional Japanese codes of behavior, once they see their value, while the Japanese sometimes find American assertiveness refreshing and are impressed by some American business practices, such as performance management, even importing them to their operations in Japan. But the cost can be high in time lost, money spent, and employees alienated. With the knowledge we now have about the nature of cross-cultural conflicts and the skills needed to mediate them, a much more rational approach is available. It is the approach we have described in detail here. This approach will produce results more rapidly at less expense and, perhaps as important, give expatriate Japanese managers the tools not only to convince headquarters of the need in their U.S. subsidiaries for changes in traditional Japanese practices but also to demonstrate their potential value as models for other operations both at home and worldwide.

Communication: The Key Factor

In the end, if there is a single most important key to interorganizational conflict resolution, it is effective communication. Assuming the communication style and the message itself are understood across cultures, then we can safely say that the more communication between headquarters and subsidiary organizations, the more likely those organizations will be able to make good decisions. But communication and understanding will not lead to conflict resolution unless accompanied by the mediation of the diverse values, assumptions, expectations, and norms inherent in the headquarters and subsidiary corporate cultures.

The true meaning of globalization lies not in continual localization but rather in finding the proper balance between what corporate headquarters sees as the essential universals of its business and what overseas subsidiaries demand in the form of local adaptations or modifications. Perhaps the most important lessons to be learned from the conflicts we have analyzed in this book are these: (1) they are often very predictable; (2) when ignored, they usually result in a loss of productivity, higher employee turnover, and even lawsuits; and (3) using the cross-cultural conflict resolution model, the disputes can be effectively resolved, ultimately helping to foster a healthy and productive relationship between headquarters, expatriate managers, and local employees in the subsidiaries.

Glossary of
Japanese Terms

Term	Definition
akachochin	Japanese neighborhood bar
amae	reciprocal dependency
atomawashi	table conflict until later
bonenkai	end-of-year office celebration
chukaisha	conflict mediator
domo sumimasen	"I'm sorry"
doryoku	demonstrated effort
enryo	hesitation, reserve
funikizukuri	change of amosphere
giri	duty
honne	true feelings

ishin denshin	tacit understanding of each other's true feelings
joshiki	common sense
kaizen	continual pursuit of perfection
karoshi	death from being overworked
kogaisha	"child" company
makete mi o toru	feigned humility to gain advantage
manga	Japanese cartoon
nemawashi	private discussions for consensus building
nintairyoku	patience
on	obligation, kindness, a favor or a debt of gratitude
oseiji	excessive or unnecessary compliments
sekinin	ultimate responsibility
Shigoto wa shikarareteiru uchi ga hana.	As long as your boss is criticizing you, it is good because he cares about you.
Shin-Jin-Rui	new generation
tatemae	diplomatic public behavior
wa	harmony

About the Authors

Clifford Clarke

G. Douglas Lipp

Clifford Clarke is the founder and CEO of Clarke Consulting Group, a global consulting and training firm located in Redwood City, California.

A founder of the intercultural field who has led the way in bridging the intercultural and business worlds, Mr. Clarke's geographic area of expertise is Japan. Clarke's family has an extensive history in that country dating back to 1898; he himself lived in Japan from the age of seven until he returned to the U.S. to attend college. He has a strong academic background in intercultural communication and cofounded and directed the Stanford Institute for Intercultural Communication.

Since 1974 Mr. Clarke's extensive experience in business has included serving as a consultant to international corporations. He has been director of research projects, conducted corporate culture studies, and facilitated technology transfers for numerous American companies with subsidiaries in Japan. He also served for many years as a consultant to Japan's Ministry of Education and its Ministry of International Trade and Industry for the design and implementation of selection and training programs.

At present, Mr. Clarke works as a consultant to senior management of a number of Japanese and American companies. He conducts specially designed sessions for senior management teams on integrated leadership, intercultural team building, and corporate culture development. Mr. Clarke's clients include Boston Scientific, Hitachi, Motorola, Procter & Gamble, and Honda.

Douglas Lipp is president of G. Douglas Lipp & Associates, an international business consulting organization. His experience includes over 20 years working as an intermediary between American and Japanese businesses. He writes and speaks extensively about the cultural and management challenges facing international managers. The consulting and training services offered by Lipp's company are designed to help American, Japanese and European multinational corporations determine culturally appropriate management styles and business strategies.

In addition, Lipp also leads economic development missions to and from Japan in order to help companies from both countries develop business partnerships.

Mr. Lipp is formerly of the Walt Disney Company and NEC Electronics. While with Disney, he was assigned to the start-up team on the Tokyo Disneyland project from preopening ramp-up to project completion. At NEC Electronics, Lipp counseled Japanese and American managers in effective cross-cultural communication skills and led strategic executive planning sessions.

Lipp has a MA degree in International Business Communication from California State University, Sacramento. He spent two years at International Christian University, Tokyo, and at Nanzan University, Nagoya, Japan, in post-graduate studies of Japanese language and history. Fluent in Japanese, he is the author of *Tokyo Disneyland: The Secret of its Success,* a Japanese publication.